Works
Well with
Others

Works Well with Others

AN OUTSIDER'S GUIDE TO SHAKING HANDS, SHUTTING UP, HANDLING JERKS, AND OTHER CRUCIAL SKILLS IN BUSINESS THAT NO ONE EVER TEACHES YOU

Ross McCammon

DUTTON
— est. 1852 —

DUTTON
— est. 1852 —
An imprint of Penguin Random House LLC
375 Hudson Street
New York, New York 10014

LIBRARY OF CONGRESS CATALOGING-IN-PUBLICATION DATA
McCammon, Ross.
Works well with others : an outsider's guide to shaking hands, shutting up, handling jerks, and other crucial skills in business that no one ever teaches you / Ross McCammon.
pages cm
Includes index.
ISBN 978-0-525-95502-3 (hardback)—ISBN 978-0-698-19434-2 (ebook)
1. Business—Humor. 2. Business etiquette—Humor. I. Title.
PN6231.B85M33 2015
818'.602—dc23
2015009498

Printed in the United States of America
10 9 8 7 6 5 4 3 2 1

Set in ITC Slimbach Std
Designed by Alissa Rose Theodor

For Nina

Contents

Contents

Contents

Contents

Works
Well with
Others

Introduction

What Are You Doing Here?

I'm going to make a few assumptions about you. If I'm wrong, I hope you'll read the rest of this book anyway. Also: I'm sorry for misreading you. If I'm right, well, I'm clearly some sort of wizard.

You look great, by the way.

Anyway, this is who I think you are. You're smart. You're talented. You're ambitious. But you're not "well-leveraged." You don't think you have an "edge" on the competition. You don't have "hookups" that you can exploit. You don't have a "stellar pedigree," as if you are some sort of racehorse. You are not the spawn of a CEO and you can't call upon the powers of nepotism when things aren't "looking up." You don't "know" a lot of "people."

You're an outsider.

And your outsider status has made you a little uncomfortable. You're not "sure of yourself" in a job interview. You don't know how to "make a presentation" or "give a speech." You're not sure what to order when you're at an "important lunch."

You're finding my use of quotation marks "kind of stupid."

It's important for you to know that all of those things describe me too. I'm pretty smart, kind of talented, and moderately ambitious, but when I unexpectedly (and, from my perspective, miraculously) got a call from *Esquire* magazine in 2005 to interview for an editor position, I felt crucially ill equipped for the job. I worked at Southwest Airlines' in-flight magazine (the *Esquire* of airplane magazines), had a degree from the University of North Texas (the Harvard of the northeastern Texas / southern Oklahoma region), and knew sort-of-important people, but they were all in Dallas (the New York City of . . . eh, never mind).

I thought that my circumstances would determine my eventual failure in New York. Because I wasn't the right type. And I didn't deserve it. I was an impostor, and I was going to be found out about a month in. **(Rule: Nothing can be found out about a person less than a month into a job. Nothing. Because you're not seeing the real person. You're seeing an agent for that person whose job it is to confusedly stare at the fancy electronic restroom faucets until someone comes along who knows how they work.)**

The term "impostor phenomenon" was coined in 1978 by Georgia State University psychologists Pauline Clance and Suzanne Imes. Initially linked mainly to high-achieving women (but later seen as often—if not more so—in men), it can be broken down into three types of feelings: that you aren't as successful as other people think; that your accomplishments can be chalked up to luck; and that even if you've attained success, it isn't all *that* impressive.

Since that initial research, psychologists have studied and debated the possible causes of "impostorism." Is it a trait or is it a state of mind? Is it a "situational condition" or is it deeply rooted in how we were parented? Is it merely a reflection of an anxious personality? Or depression? Are people who describe themselves as frauds actually more confident than they let on, as some researchers have suggested? Is it a "self-presentational strategy"—something that people do, consciously or not, to seem extra humble or to lower others' expectations of them?

This book isn't so concerned with *why* people feel like impostors but that people *do.*

And a lot of people do.

People like Supreme Court Justice Sonia Sotomayor: "My first month as a judge I was terrified. . . . I still couldn't believe this had worked out as dreamed, and I felt myself almost an impostor meeting my fate so brazenly."

And Kate Winslet: "Sometimes I wake up in the morning before going off to a shoot, and I think, I can't do this. I'm a fraud."

And Chuck Lorre, creator/writer/producer of *The Big Bang Theory* and *Two and a Half Men:* "When you go and watch a rehearsal of something you've written and it stinks, the natural feeling is 'I stink. I'm a fraud. I need to go and hide.'"

And Alexis Ohanian, cofounder of Reddit: "I have no idea what I'm doing, and that's awesome."

And Tina Fey: "You just try to ride the egomania when it comes and enjoy it, and then slide through the idea of fraud."

And Meryl Streep: "You think, 'Why would anyone want to see me again in a movie? And I don't know how to act anyway, so why am I doing this?'"

When I got to New York, I felt unlike all of my peers. I didn't dress the part. I didn't know anyone important. I didn't know how to have a business lunch. I didn't even really know how to order a drink in a bar. (At this point, you may be questioning my ability to clean and feed myself. Bear with me.) I didn't know how to work at a big magazine and I didn't know how to live in a city like New York.

But a few months after working in New York, a truth came into focus: Everyone around me was an impostor, too. We all have insecurities. And I think successful people are successful *because* of them. Not in spite of them. There's great energy in the spot on the Venn diagram where awkwardness and ambition overlap. There's a great energy in weirdness.

Hugely important rule: Everyone is weird and nervous. No matter how famous or important, everyone is just really weird and really nervous. Especially the people who don't seem weird or nervous.

I came to see that the difference between those who are successful and those who aren't isn't just talent or behavior. The people I came to respect the most weren't any better minds or workers than I was (though they were talented and hardworking, believe me). They were just better at *seeming* better. They acted like they belonged. They seemed to claim success by performing its mechanics with confidence.

And as I met more and more interesting people (from people in my industry to famous actors and musicians as a part of my job), I began to realize that most of the so-called rules of success don't work. You don't have to "sell" yourself. You don't have to "network." And you don't have to dress the "right" way (although that has its advantages). But you do have to understand why people do those things. And you have to comport yourself with integrity, even when you have no idea what's going on—in the meeting room, at a business lunch, or at the bar after work.

I also learned that the problem is not being ignorant of certain customs or devoid of certain skills. The problem is letting your inadequacies get to you.

This is a book about success, but my angle on success is a sideways one. I am not going to spell out any sort of "system" or "philosophy." This is a self-help book for people who don't like self-help books. It's less concerned with how to "get" a job than how to interview for one. It's less concerned with how to overcome a fear of public speaking than how to approach a podium. To borrow a now-overused construct from the military, this book is less concerned about strategy than it is about tactics. It's not about the "what." It's about the "how" and the "who."

This book is about the seemingly small things, which are important for three reasons: The small things can cause crippling anxiety when you don't think you have a handle on them. (This kind of anxiety is totally unnecessary.) The small things are emblematic of greatness, signals to others that you are not messing around, code for integrity, dedication, and consideration. The small things are of huge *practical* importance—they're what make other people feel comfortable around you, make an immediate impression, and cover up mistakes.

For my entire career, I've been obsessed with how the small things—from an amusing turn of phrase in a magazine story to a handshake at the beginning of a business lunch—are often the most memorable things and can add up to something very big. And important. And lucrative.

Impostorism is not something to overcome. It's not

something to "fake" your way out of. You can't "fake it to make it." No, you need to harness your fear to work for you. Embrace your outsider status. Embrace your mistakes. Success is about being a human being, not a drone. But in order to seem human you have to reckon with the small customs of professional life—even if you eventually reject their importance to you.

It's possible to use small but meaningful moments to feel and seem comfortable even when you don't think you belong.

But you do. Of course you do.

1

First, a Little Story

Monday, May 16, 2005

On the second floor of the northeast wing of a big office building in the middle of a nondescript business park in the suburbs between Dallas and Fort Worth, I arrived back at my desk after lunch. I was a young editor in chief of *Spirit*, the in-flight magazine of Southwest Airlines. My lunch was a number one value size from Chick-fil-A, eaten in my car while driving back to the office. My state was vaguely dissatisfied—both with my fried-chicken sandwich and with my job at an in-flight magazine in the suburbs of Dallas.

Placed conspicuously upon my keyboard was a message. There was the name of a person I didn't recognize, the name of a media company I *did* recognize, and a New York phone number.

This was odd, because the company was Hearst—a major media corporation based in New York. Hearst owned *Cosmopolitan, Marie Claire, Good Housekeeping, Popular*

Mechanics, Esquire, and lots of other "major newsstand" magazines.

So I called the guy back.

"I'm the recruiting director for Hearst Magazines, I'm looking for candidates for an open editor position, and I'd love to talk with you about it," he said.

Which was a strange thing to hear. Now, I had a pretty good job. Of the nine or ten in-flight magazines in the United States, mine was certainly among the top, oh, seven. And at thirty, I was objectively successful. But while I was in the media, I was in a minor part of the media. If *Esquire* was the big dance, *Spirit* magazine was smoking pot behind the gym.

So it struck me as strange that the recruiter would want to talk to me. Turns out he had been on a Southwest Airlines flight from Philadelphia to Pittsburgh over the weekend, had pulled the in-flight magazine from the seatback pocket in front of him, had actually read it, and had thought that it wasn't bad.

My first thought was "This could be big." My second thought was "There's probably been some mistake." My third thought was "There's definitely been some mistake."

There's a thing that happens to me when the odor of opportunity floats my way. It triggers a combination of giddiness and revulsion. (Outkast once remarked, "Don't everybody like the smell of gasoline?" That's how I feel about opportunity. Alternately pleasing and repellant.) Which describes my general state for the duration of the phone call. Over the course of about fifteen minutes, the recruiter asked me a lot of pointed questions about my career and my magazine. His end of the conversation was appropriately cryptic. Due to the general sense of discretion that aids in a recruiter's work (as well as federal anti-discrimination laws that forbid certain kinds of questions during all job interviews), all screening conversations are like this.

After about twenty minutes of a one-sided conversation, I finally asked the recruiter a question.

"What's this about?"

If you could somehow look at my brain's thought log from that day, there would be a span lasting about two-thirds of a second in which there were forty-five instances of the thought, "Please say *Esquire.*"

"There's a job at *Esquire*," he said.

Now, because I am pathologically incapable of fully embracing an obviously positive professional development, likely due to a genetic defense mechanism inherited from a long line of humble, hardscrabble, frequently disappointed ancestors from Texas and Kentucky, I immediately thought that the whole thing was a scam. An involuntary psychological girding occurred. The odor of opportunity became a stench. I typed "magazine hiring scam" into Google. This situation was a little too *Trading Places*-esque for my liking. This guy was Don Ameche, the editor in chief was Ralph Bellamy, and I was Eddie Murphy rolling around on a furniture dolly, pretending to have no legs and begging for money. I wondered if I was being "punk'd" (to use a phrase that not only dates me but makes it seem like I used to watch MTV's *Punk'd* hosted by Ashton Kutcher, which I did, but still).

"The lousy bastards," I recall muttering away from the phone. (Note: I almost certainly didn't mutter "The lousy bastards" away from the phone.)

The moment he said *"Esquire"* I remembered that one of the many questions he'd asked me earlier in the conversation was, "If you could work at any magazine at Hearst, which magazine would it be?" (This is a typical recruiter question—forces you to either qualify or disqualify yourself.) I'd said, *"Esquire,"* in the same way Oliver Twist says, "Please, sir, I want some more."

And so, armed with deep skepticism, I responded like . . . an excitable schoolboy.

"Really?!"

"Could you come to New York next Monday?" he said.

Esquire had been my favorite magazine for years. It was the magazine I modeled my own magazine after. Working there was a dream I'd never allowed myself to have. "This will end in utter failure," I thought. "If I don't get rejected after the editor in chief reads my résumé and sees that I went to a school with a name involving a cardinal direction, I will screw up this interview like no one has ever screwed up an interview. I will spill coffee on the editor in chief's desk. I will forget to wear socks." (Years later, I would find out that socklessness is considered a virtue by people in fashion.) "I will improbably mispronounce '*Esquire*' as 'es-QUIRE,' as if I am Javier Bardem. I will inexplicably urinate on a plant.

"Even worse, I will forget everybody's name, talk too fast, and screw up the handshakes."

This kind of auto-psych-out is routine for me. I never feel "up to the task." I feel "at war with the task." I feel like the task is taunting me, reminding me that I grew up in a neighborhood in Dallas supposedly on the wrong side of the tracks; that I played lot of ragtag neighborhood games when I was a kid but never competed in an organized way; that I made terrible grades in school; that every day of my seventh-grade year I was literally kicked in the ass by a kid whose name I didn't know and who never said a word to me; that my mom—who raised me as a single mom from the time I was three months old—took me out of what she considered a dangerous public school where a mute kid could daily kick her son's ass unchecked and put me into a tiny evangelical private school simply because it was near our home; that my teachers there constantly "prayed for me" because I didn't seem to be "accepting Jesus as my personal Lord and

Savior"; that my graduating class had only eight people in it—eight!; that, despite my terrible grades, I was the salutatorian in that class of eight people—salutatorian!—but that I was only "acting" salutatorian because the kid who earned the spot was kicked out of school for behavior reasons right before graduation; that I went to the University of *North* Texas, not the University of Texas; that I worked at an inflight magazine, not a newsstand magazine; that even despite my automatically privileged status as a random white guy, I've always felt like I was in the second or third tier and never the first. Ever. The recruiter, who represented the big stage, was talking to someone who'd never been on the big stage. I was never part of the main thing. I was always part of the other thing. Challenges like going to New York that Monday only highlighted my class B status.

(Fortunately for my career, when I am faced with a challenge, my reaction is fight, not flight.)

Despite the near certainty of those failures of comportment that surely awaited me—at a magazine that is an authority on comportment!—I gave him the only answer I could possibly give, the answer we all must give when opportunity calls us up and seems to taunt us by asking if we are bold enough to become more successful: "You shittin' me?"

I eventually said something that meant yes, because a week later, I was leaning against the wall of Merchants'

Gate at the southwest corner of Central Park, across from Columbus Circle, a block away from the magazine's offices, on a beautiful Monday morning in May, reviewing ten pages of responses to possible interview questions that I'd hand-written the night before, and feeling like I was a character in a lesser Nora Ephron movie.

I was very early. I was wearing my nicest shoes. I was wearing a tie. I was—

Wait a minute. I wasn't wearing a suit jacket.

I should've been wearing a jacket.

Why wasn't I wearing a jacket?

2

Should You Keep Reading This Book?

Circle each answer that applies, and add up the points to find out if you should stick with this.

Which word best describes how you read the first two chapters?

Devoured (5)

Skimmed (4)

Used as makeshift umbrella (2)

When you walk into a room, which type of gait are you most likely to exhibit?

Swagger (0)

Mosey (3)

A slink-type deal (5)

Is your alma mater part of the Ivy League?

Yes (–8)

No (2)

If your alma mater is part of the Ivy League, are its buildings actually covered in ivy?

Yes (–15)

No (0)

Are you aware of any of the following? Circle all that apply.

What color your parachute is (–4)

Where your cheese might be (–4)

Whether you're leaning in or leaning out (–4)

Which of the following have you accidentally said in a professional situation instead of saying "Thank you" because of anxiety?

"You're welcome." (2)

"Thank welcome." (4)

"You're you." (6)

Which of the following do you regularly do at work?

Chew your fingernails (3)

Weep (4)

Weep while chewing your fingernails (10)

You're hired!

"I knew it!" (–7)

"Oh shit." (5)

Quick: Draw a boat that represents you on your professional journey.

Which kind of boat is that up there?

Yacht (0)

Cruise ship (–10)

Dinghy (4)

One of those banana things they got in the Caribbean (7)

Draw a boat? How is this helping me? (-30)

Which is the most useful professional tool?

Ambition (–5)

Competitiveness (–6)

Eye contact (4)

Staple remover (0)

Backup staple remover (0)

Which best describes your mouth right now?

Smile (0)

Robotic grin (–3)

Frown (10)

Indifferent simper (5)

Were you simpering before you read the previous question and then you smiled?

How'd you know?! (15)

No. (0)

Let's do this!

All right! (35)

I'm not smiling. (0)

How 'bout now?

OK, maybe a little. (10)

KEY

Fewer than 0 points: There is absolutely no reason for you to continue reading this book. But your nephew Matt? Right up his alley.

1–20 points: You should skip around.

More than 20 points: You skipped this quiz and are currently reading the next chapter.

3

How to Be Interviewed

Why it never occurred to me to wear a jacket to my *Esquire* interview I don't know. Today, I can't imagine being without one. For me, a suit jacket or sport coat is a protector, an organizer, and a cloak for a wrinkled shirt. And it is obviously the right thing to wear to a job interview at *Esquire* and any other workplace involving four walls, a kitchenette, and people who almost certainly wore jackets to *their* interviews.

I came from an office park in Texas. No one wore a full suit or even a sport coat with jeans. You wore a button-down shirt and pants to work. Maybe you tucked in. *Maybe.*

That I was a walking "fashion don't" dawned on me as I was signing my name in the register at the front desk of 1790 Broadway.

My anxiety grew as I took a creaky elevator up to the thirteenth floor. (Thirteenth!)

It fully blossomed as I emerged from the elevator and

was confronted with a framed poster-size cover of the June 2005 issue of *Esquire,* which featured Ewan McGregor. He appeared to be staring me down.

And then, swear to god: McGregor shook his head with pity.

And then, swear to god: One of the cover lines morphed into: "Putz Doesn't Wear Suit Jacket to Interview. Let's See How This Goes!"

And then I was buzzed in.

My first two interviews were with the number two and number three staffers at *Esquire:* the deputy editor and the editorial director. They were two of the best conversations I've ever had. The energy was right. There was chemistry. I talked and they listened. They talked and I listened. They seemed normal. They weren't marked by elitism or dismissiveness. They were warm, interested. They were affable.

My anxiety about clothes began to go away. The substance of the conversations was too distracting.

As the conversations went on, I gathered that their jobs were to clear my personality. There was a lot of small talk. A lot of prompts, not a lot of questioning.

So you work at an airplane magazine?

Do you enjoy living in Texas?

You don't like suit jackets? (They didn't ask this question.)

My demeanor was suddenly marked by enthusiasm. And I became something that we're not supposed to be when we're interviewing for a job: Honest. And authentic.

I was relaxed.

After the second interview, I walked to a Greek restaurant a few blocks away to have lunch with the recruiting director who'd called me a week earlier. The meal was memorable mostly because I managed to order four courses of dishes involving phyllo.

"Big fan of puff pastry?" the recruiter asked.

"Huge," I said.

Wow.

On our way out, he said to me, "Don't strain your neck looking at all the tall buildings."

"This guy thinks I'm a yokel," I thought. And then I looked around and said to myself, "These really are some tall buildings."

I don't remember much of the meeting with the editor in chief. I remember thinking that it was nice of him to pull up a chair in front of his desk and sit down, which made the playing field a little more level. I remember being asked what recent books I liked. I remember saying *The Tipping Point* even though I'd read only a quarter of it. I remember saying, "I've only read about a quarter of it," and thinking that I sounded like an idiot. I remember being asked if I watched TV. "Yes," I said.

Brilliant.

I remember profanity. At first it was jarring. And then it became comfortable. As if we were just hanging out, having a conversation in a bar. Not only was it a substantive conversation, it was a pleasure. That I didn't feel qualified for the job or prepared for its social demands, that I wasn't wearing a jacket . . . all of that went away.

I got the impression that I could have been wearing shorts, and if I was what he was looking for, then I was what he was looking for.

I became comfortable enough toward the end to say, "Look, if you throw me out of your office right now, this will have been the best thing that's ever happened to me."

(And I can tell you, ten years later, having interviewed and been interviewed, this is exactly the kind of thing you want to say. It's got everything a prospective boss wants: humility, candor, enthusiasm, and gratitude.)

I left elated. Not because I thought I would get the job, but because I had a great story to tell people when I got home. And because I was in the offices of my favorite magazine for a few hours. I was honored to have been considered. I was grateful for the experience. And I was relieved that something as superficial as what I was wearing didn't seem to make a difference.

I walked back to my hotel on Forty-Seventh Street to gather my luggage. I needed to catch a plane in a couple of hours. I figured I would hear back in a week or so. Or maybe never again.

And then, less than forty-five minutes after my interview ended, my cell phone rang.

212- . . .

That's New York.

649- . . .

That's *Esquire.*

I answered the phone thinking someone would tell me that, funny thing, they'd meant to call young hotshot editor Reese McDrummond and the whole thing had been a complete misunderstanding.

It was the editor in chief.

"I'd like you to come work at *Esquire,*" he said.

Please count to five before reading the next sentence.

. . .

That's how long I didn't speak after being offered the job. Which is a long time to not say something. I suffered from temporary locked-in syndrome. It was like the paralysis you have right before you bungee-jump or the pause that happens right before you volunteer to sing your first karaoke song of the night when you're still sober enough to be aware of how much you're about to corrupt the Bee Gees' "How Deep Is Your Love" (sung with the eyes closed and two hands on the mic, as is my style). It was a kind of mini-stroke.

The silence was interrupted by "I'm really surprised." (At least that's what I think I said.)

"Think about it for a while. Call me back."

The next thing I remember was calling my mom from an airport bar and trying not to cry.

Some flights out of LaGuardia go right down the length of Manhattan, as if the pilot just decides, "I don't care what the tower says, Johnson. We're taking the scenic route!" As if on cue, the flight back to DFW was one of them. The moment was excruciatingly poignant: a first-class upgrade for some reason, which afforded me a couple of free drinks before takeoff, a sunset that looked like the painted backdrop from a fifties Western, a dude next to me who wouldn't stop talking to me so I could focus on how poignant it all was, a job offer that would allow me to live and work in New York City, the full measure of which I could see out my window.

What an amazing and unlikely view.

4

Classic Interview Rules, Plus One More

Despite the existence of the book you're reading, I am generally skeptical about very specific career advice. Business guidelines about social matters can sometimes make us robotic and just like everyone else. Authenticity and candor are crucial virtues in the workplace—and underrated virtues for interviews. Looking back, I'm glad I was myself during the interview. But behavior tips are important, if only because they can alleviate anxiety going in.

Here Are the Classic Rules That Most Sources of Interview Advice Agree Are Crucial:

Research the employer. Find out what they've done and where they seem to be headed.

Practice your answers.

Come equipped with extra copies of your résumés and references, samples of your work, and a pen and note-pad.

Have a response to "Tell me about yourself."

Have a response to the "What's your greatest weakness?" question, which should not be "I try too hard" or some other humble brag. (Focus on skills that have needed improvement but that you have started to improve.)

Answer questions with specific examples.

Show you're the right fit. Detail how your experience matches up with the specific job description.

Have your own questions ready.

Don't talk money.

Send a thank-you note. Handwritten is better than email.

All great advice, but the thing that interview experts rarely address is deception. Never pretend you're something you're not. Jobs aren't to be *gotten*. Jobs are to be matched to. The biggest flameouts I've ever seen are people who were one person during their interview and a different person once they were in the job. Skill can be taught. Personality is something you're stuck with. Your coworkers and boss are stuck with it too.

And at some point toward the end of the interview, consider saying, "If you throw me out of here right now, this will have been the greatest thing that's ever happened to me." It works. As long as you believe it.

5

How to Talk to a Recruiter

I've always found recruiter interviews to be more fraught than prospective employer interviews. 1. They always ask questions you can't say no to. ("Are you interested in taking the next step in your career?") 2. They immediately want extremely personal information from you. ("So what are you making?") 3. And they end the conversation cryptically, almost meaninglessly, as if they are either high-level diplomats at a treaty negotiation or someone you met on Match and had a weird first date with . . . or a high-level diplomat you met on Match ("So now you know a little bit about what I'm looking for. I know a little bit about what you're looking for. Let's see how this goes.") There's a lot more covert digging and discreet maneuvering going on with a recruiter interview than with a prospective-employer interview. My interview with the recruiter was typical: intriguing but a little confusing.

Recruiters aren't only looking to help an employer fill a

slot. They're interested in starting a relationship. They know that this might not be the right fit but that in the future another job might come along that is. Recruiters look at their conversations with you as fact-gathering missions. They want to know about you. But they also want to know about where you work—what kinds of salaries people make there and the organization's hierarchical structure. This information becomes part of the tapestry of intelligence they have on your industry and who works in it.

As I was writing this book almost ten years after that first phone call, I had lunch with a top New York–based media-industry recruiter to discuss something that doesn't get enough attention: the recruiters' role in your career.

These are the rules and suggestions that I gleaned from that lunch, which marked the first time I've ever had a conversation with a recruiter that wasn't marked by a strange combination of amiableness and ambiguity.

Don't be late. It's fine if it happens, but, really, try to not be late.

Use the recruiter to get information on the hiring manager. Because hiring managers tend to want someone either exactly like them or the exact opposite. This will be useful if you get to interview with the hiring manager.

Give the recruiter information on your workplace that they can add to their file on your current employer. This will endear you to them. It's one of the reasons they're meeting with you.

Do not use them *just* to get a counteroffer. They will know what's going on and will never call you again.

Give them the real story of your career. Be candid. Tell your *actual* story. If you're right for the job, that story's next chapter will be the job the recruiter is trying to fill.

Don't bad-mouth your current employer. The recruiter knows and likes people there, and you will seem small.

Talk about how you can contribute to the new place, not what the new place will contribute to your career.

Talk less about your greatest hits and obvious weaknesses and more about the stuff in between.

Don't ask about the recruiter's life or career. The subject is you. It's OK to seem self-obsessed during a recruiter interview.

Send a thank-you note to the recruiter.

But no gifts. It's excessive. Like you're trying to make up for some professional deficiency.

And, really: Don't be late.

6

How to Enter a Room

Looking back at my interview, I see that much of my anxiety revolved around simply *arriving*. In the days leading up to the interview, I was concerned about the first impression I'd make. The realization in the elevator that I wasn't appropriately dressed only exacerbated the anxiety. And at the worst possible time.

Within the last decade there's been lots of studies on first impressions. Most of them show that our anxieties aren't unfounded. First impressions are highly influential, and not just in the short term.

When it comes to meeting people in an interview setting—when it comes to making first impressions—you begin winning or losing very early on. Like—very, very, very early on. Earlier. No, even earlier.

Research suggests that people will form an impression of you within *milliseconds* of seeing your face for the first time and that this is what will work in your favor: gregariousness, friendliness, assertiveness, social skill, verbal skill, eye contact, evidence of emotional stability, and agreeableness. Not: shyness, shrinking, running away, screaming, and running away while screaming.

The fact is that we are animals, constantly sniffing around, constantly looking out for threats, but also looking for allies; that we make impressions extremely early, probably because that's what it's taken for us to survive as a species. We are fawns at the edge of the forest, looking over there. And over there. And over there! And . . . hey, man, let's get back in the woods where it's safe.

But unlike the deer and the meerkats and the woodchucks, we form first impressions that are extremely nuanced. We're not just judging threats—we're judging warmth, trustworthiness, confidence, social dominance . . . whether or not someone is a fastidious personal groomer. We're very good at getting first impressions, at knowing whether or not we will "like" or "dislike" someone.

Clearly, this is a massive opportunity.

Now, about entering a room . . .

Entering a room is easy. Assuming you're on time and you know exactly what you want from the people in the room and you know their names and you've Googled them and found out where they went to school and that according to LinkedIn they made a couple of questionable professional moves in the early 2000s and all of them tweet.

The main problem with entering an unfamiliar meeting room is that it's like leaving a bar when it's still light outside. Things seem a little too bright, a little overwhelming, a little disconcerting. It's like you're in a kind of parallel universe but you have no idea where the restrooms are. Yet no matter how thrown off you feel, the guiding principle is: It's your room. For the next, oh, thirty seconds to a minute, you're in charge. Even if it's their room, you're in charge. Even if your salary is one-hundredth of the salary of that guy you're about to shake hands with, you're in charge. You're not the only one determining the mood of the room, but you have to take responsibility for it.

Here is where I will introduce a rule that will apply to every subsequent chapter: **Eye contact. Do not look down, to the side, through them, at their chest, into their souls. Look everyone in the eye.** Studies show that interview candidates who maintain a high level of eye contact are judged much more favorably than those who don't. Eye contact is a crucial determinant of interview success.

Through eye contact we gather information, give or receive cues about how to act and when to speak, and express intimacy (even in a professional setting). People tend to look away from a questioner when asked a difficult question. A shift in gaze can indicate personal discomfort, uncertainty, lack of control. People who are in control and feel confident and fluent about the subject being discussed tend to maintain eye contact.

And it's not merely eye contact. The *gaze* is crucial—during interviews, keeping eye contact at least half the time will make you seem more competent and confident. Look at yourself in the mirror and hold your gaze for a second before glancing away. Now do it for five seconds. You will trust the second version of you more than the first. You will feel more comfortable with that version. You may wink at it even. The important part is that you will like yourself the longer you gaze. (But not too long. There's a fine line between gazing and staring and an even finer line between staring and menacing. The line between menacing and freaking people out is even finer.)

So look people in the eye. Before you shake their hands, before you smile even.

Because what you're suggesting is the most underrated virtue of business: curiosity. I don't think there's a virtue in business more underrated. If you're curious about something, or even better, some*one*, you establish a crucial foundation for the meeting. And it's important to set the tone early—even if it's not about the business at hand. Most of my meetings at *Esquire* start off with questions about the view from our conference room on the twenty-first floor of the Hearst Tower in Midtown. If the person I'm meeting with asks anything at all about the city, I take them over to the window and give them a quick tour of what you can see: the expanse of low buildings that make up Hell's Kitchen, the exact location in the Hudson where Captain Sully landed the plane, that statue of a decapitated Ronald McDonald that has sat upright in a chair on the roof of a four-floor walk-up on Eighth Avenue for seven years, how New Jersey looks almost bucolic if you squint. Almost. It's a rich, interesting conversation. Because it was spurred by curiosity.

Who wouldn't want to be in a room with you now? You're amiable and confident and pleased with the way things are going. You're someone the other people in the room could see themselves doing business with.

And you haven't even sat down yet.

7

How to Have a First Day on the Job

I wish I had read the preceding chapter before my first day at *Esquire.*

The problem wasn't that I wasn't acting gregarious and agreeable. The problem was that I wasn't aware of just how gregarious and agreeable I was acting. When I'm excited and nervous, I do what many of us do: I behave not like myself but like some caricature of myself. I overdo it. I say too much at a party. I ask people slightly impertinent questions that I'm not all that interested in the answers to.

And apparently, I enthusiastically introduce myself to strangers in the men's room.

My life had been pretty intense leading up to my first day at *Esquire.* I was offered the job on a Monday. I accepted on a Friday. (Note: This is too long to wait to accept a job offer. I'm not sure what I was thinking here. I suppose I was trying to buy time since I knew my new boss wanted me to start as soon as possible and I had a lot of loose ends to tie up at home and arrangements to make in New York.) I flew up to New York to find an apartment a week after that. After seeing five places in the Village during a single afternoon, I took the fifth apartment—a fourth-floor walk-up a block north of Washington Square Park on West Eighth Street. The apartment was situated over a store, L'Impasse, which specialized in articles of clothing that can best be described as evening wear for discerning strippers. Despite the drawbacks, I took it: not because I liked it but because it was the only place I saw that didn't have a toilet in the kitchen or some other impractical layout unique to Downtown Manhattan real estate and because it was the last apartment I saw and I had to make a decision. (Looking back, I can see it was a great place. Plenty big, a view straight down MacDougal Street, and a great location—I could actually see a few feet of the Washington Square Arch. But that Sunday afternoon, I barely had time to assess its virtues.)

My friend Craig and I had left Dallas on a Thursday, staying over in Knoxville, Tennessee, and then Princeton, New Jersey, before rolling into New York early on a Saturday morning. The city was quiet. All the storefronts on West Eighth were closed, their security gates locked tight. It looked desolate and sad—like a scene in *Taxi Driver*. We spent a day moving in. Every time I went downstairs to get another load, the street was more crowded. L'Impasse's explicitly sexual background music was a little louder. And, in the heat of summer, everything smelled a little more pungent.

Turns out I had chosen a lively, if not particularly homey, block.

On Sunday morning, Craig and I walked downstairs. He was leaving for his flight; I was going to go do whatever people in New York do on a warm Sunday morning: Read the *Times* in Washington Square Park? Eat, like, a bagel, and, uh, lox? Seem irritated for no reason? As we pushed on the first set of doors, we felt resistance. The door wasn't locked, but there was something preventing us from opening it. We looked down to see a large mass of clothing and a hand languidly waving us away. There was a large person of indeterminate gender somehow situated *in between* the two sets of locked doors you had to walk through to get inside the apartment building.

We stepped over the person, carefully, and then we emerged from the building onto the sidewalk and looked at each other as if to say, "What the hell was that?" (In the coming months, I would not be so careful when this happened, and it happened a few times that first year. I came to say loudly, "Good morning!" And "Go away!" And "I'm sorry, sir or madam, but, I mean, come on!")

The four L'Impasse mannequins behind the large plate-glass window, with their arms akimbo, their risqué frocks, and their lack of defined facial features, seemed only to mock us.

As I walked around the neighborhood by myself for the first time, I noticed that there were now a *lot* of people milling about. Some of them had lawn chairs, which seemed peculiar. Barriers had been set up on either side of Eighth Street, and a purple line had been painted down the middle of the road as if marking a route.

The throngs got big enough that once I was back upstairs I Googled "8th Street June 26 event."

Turns out it was the culmination of Gay Pride Week, which celebrates the struggle for gay rights and which is most notable for its colorful parade from Midtown to the West Village, which apparently was a few hours away from cavalcading down my block.

"Cool," I thought, "a parade." A thing that everyone famously loves. And gay rights. I support those! What I didn't realize is that this parade would involve being trapped in my apartment and being forced to listen to very loud dance music for four hours. This took a while for me to realize, though. It was a slow build, starting off with— wait a minute—is that . . . ?

Hey, look, it's US senator Hillary Clinton!

And US senator Chuck Schumer!

And New York mayor Mike Bloomberg!

And there's a guy with a dog collar and a leather Speedo simulating sex with a woman in the crowd who seems to be OK with that!

As float after float, dignitary after dignitary, rights group after rights group, cause after cause, banana hammock after banana hammock, rolled by my apartment, I thought, "Oh, now I get it. Bears are hairy, too." And then I thought, "Everything is different now." Not just my surroundings. But my life. Everything.

I didn't feel lost, though. I didn't feel at home either. I felt like I was in a portal, still moving between Dallas and New York.

Everyone in the crowd, Hillary, Chuck, Mike, the four mannequins, and that dude still air humping away, all seemed to be saying, "Welcome to New York, pal. And good luck tomorrow."

So for my first morning at my new job, I was a little, uh, antsy.

Which may have been why I came to find myself shaking hands with a stranger in the men's room before even stepping into the offices.

The encounter went like this:

[Two men at the urinals.]

Hi!

Hi.

[I flush. Start washing my hands.]

I'm Ross.

Bob.

[Bob flushes. Starts washing his hands.]

It's my first day.

Oh?

Yeah.

I'm the research director at Esquire.

Ah.

[As we're drying off our hands, I reach out to shake Bob's hand. Without any alternative and with a bemused expression, Bob shakes my hand.]

Now, there are many unwritten social rules for the men's room at the office: You may look north-south, not east-west. No fine grooming. And no shaking of hands in the restroom. At any time, but especially on the morning of your first day at work.

I felt both out of place and keyed up. And when I'm nervous I tend to move quickly. When I'm speaking, I tend to start walking to the podium before I'm finished being introduced. At an important lunch, I tend to eat too fast. And, apparently, I introduce myself to coworkers in the men's room before I've even arrived at my desk.

The rest of the day was just as awkward. All first days are.

I was introduced to everyone via the classic—and re-markably ineffective—first-day walk-around.

John, this is Ross.

Hi.

Hi.

Steve, this is Ross.

Hi.

Hi.

David, this is Ross.

Hi.

Hi.

As I was shaking one of my fellow editor's hands, he actually looked me up and down. It was like something out of a bad movie about someone starting at a magazine in New York. "That's what you thought you'd wear to your first day?" this guy seemed to say. Apparently, black pants, square-toed shoes, and one of those weird collared polo shirts without buttons on the placket were not on the approved first-day attire list. (This *would* be the kind of guy who would know what a *placket* was. Jerk.)

When I sat down in my office for the first time, with no work to do and only a braille edition of *Playboy* to keep me company (it was left by my predecessor and now bestselling author A.J. Jacobs, along with a very thoughtful note and a drawer full of approximately $450 in loose change), I thought that things were off to a disheartening start. Handshake in the men's room. Awkward walk-around. Got the once-over from a coworker. It wasn't awful. First days rarely are. It was just demoralizing (which first days *often* are).

But first days are *always* some variation of this. We don't think we make a good impression. We second-guess the decision to take the job. We feel judged. We feel inadequate.

The thing is: The first day is an anomaly. And pretty much irrelevant. You say hello to all your coworkers. But that's not something you will ever do again. You stare at the fancy faucet in the restroom because you don't know it's activated by a sensor. But you'll never stare at the faucet again. You pretend to read emails that aren't there. You accidentally walk into a glass partition. You have a million notepads but no pens. You have no idea where the supply closet is and don't want to ask. You keep screwing up your out-of-office greeting and when you finally give up on it and hang up the phone, you realize that seven people within earshot now think you are obviously incompetent at arguably the most basic task of business. You stare at the salt and pepper packets in your top drawer for, like, five minutes, alternating between wanting to throw them out because they're technically other people's food and wanting to hang on to them because even lunch at your desk should be well seasoned. Little that happens on the first day is indicative of the workplace, the people who work there, or the job itself. It's like a confusing, meandering preface to an otherwise compelling book.

That's not even you walking around. That's your representative.

And those aren't your coworkers. Those are *their* representatives. We're all playing parts. People we take a shine to immediately turn out to be assholes. And the people who seem to be judging us eventually become key allies.

We think that we are the only ones filled with anxiety. But our new coworkers are anxious too. They don't know you. They don't know you don't talk too much in a meeting.

They don't know you're not a cancerous presence. They don't know you don't want their jobs. They don't know you're not gonna be crowding the fridge with your twelve-day juice cleanse.

And you don't know what they're up to either.

You end up engaging in what psychologists call "mirroring"—either consciously or subconsciously. So no one is talking? Then I won't talk. People are leaving for lunch? Then I will leave. She is making copies? Then I will make copies. That guy seems to be shunned by the tribe. Then I shall shun him . . . Wait a minute . . . Nope, they are accepting of him. *Hello, friend!*

The point is: You're not yourself.

Looking back at that first day now, I can see just how wrong I was about pretty much all of it. Ultimately it was uneventful. First days almost always are. And there might be "events," but you can't possibly know what the true meaning of the events is. It's like starting a jigsaw and seeing an image in the unconnected pieces. **The first day is simply a rite of passage. It represents so much but indicates so little.**

So the last thing you should be is nervous.

At the end of my first day, I put my feet up on the radiator in my office and looked out the window. Through the scaffolding and netting that shrouded the old twenty-story office building (which housed the magazine before it moved to the Hearst Tower in 2006), and in between two apartment buildings, I could see a narrow rectangle of green. The city seemed lonely to me; the office seemed cold to me; the May 1999 issue of *Playboy* in braille seemed like a missed opportunity to me—why not outline the Playmate in raised dots?—but the verdant expanse of Central Park seemed like pure hope . . . even if I could see only a sliver of it.

As I was soaking up the moment, my boss came by and said, "Ready for dinner?"

"Great," I said.

Let me tell you: I was not ready for dinner.

8

Ways in Which You Must Screw Up Early On: A Handy Checklist

You want to screw up. If you don't screw up when you start out, then you are overqualified for the position. Because if it was anything less than a big opportunity that affords you a ton of growth, then you would know how to do everything that's required. That it feels overwhelming—that you make loads of mistakes—lets you know that you took a big step, that you're learning things, that you're being challenged. Little failures are how you know you're succeeding.

Once, say, ten of these things have been checked off . . . congratulations, you're on your way!

☐ Reach out to shake an important person's hand in inappropriate circumstances. Such as:
- while they are eating food
- while they are in the middle of a conversation with someone else
- in a restroom

☐ Pretend you are intimately aware of something that you actually know nothing about and keep speaking about it until your ignorance becomes obvious.

☐ Conspicuously avoid making eye contact with someone you admire because you are either blinded by their glory or cowed by their power.

☐ SPEAK VERY LOUDLY *DUE TO ANXIETY.*

☐ Really screw up a presentation. By, say, forgetting how to swallow your own saliva.

☐ Loiter around a group of people at a party.

☐ Then sidle up to them.

☐ Then insert yourself into the conversation awkwardly.

☐ Use the phrase "first-day jitters" on your first day.

☐ Feel like you want to go home—home being a metaphor for any metaphorical place that possibly involves being metaphorically tucked into a metaphorical bed.

☐ Glare at your own reflection in the mirror as if you want to fight yourself.

☐ Attribute your first big accomplishment to luck and deception.

☐ Due to fatigue and intimidation, clam up at dinner on
your first day at work with all of your new colleagues,
including your boss. Like, clam up. Like, do not say
anything. For more on this, see next chapter.

9

What to Say When Someone Asks for Your Take on the Oeuvre of Werner Herzog at Dinner with Your Brand-New Colleagues and You Don't Know Who Werner Herzog Is

Y ou would think that at thirty years old, I would know how to navigate an awkward dinner full of people who intimidated me and cultural references I didn't understand. But, it turns out, I did not know how to do that.

As the entire senior staff of the magazine sat down to a large table in a private room of some just-opened Midtown restaurant that is no longer there, I felt deeply uncomfortable. And deeply intimidated. I was the guest of honor, but I didn't feel like I'd done anything worth honoring. I'd accepted a job and moved to a new city. People do that all the time. And I felt underserving of the job and the dinner.

I didn't know if people wanted me there. I didn't know if my boss was the only one who thought I belonged. I didn't know if my hiring had upset some balance.

I worried about this stuff. We all do. I now know that I should not have worried about this stuff. I now know that the best way to enter a new job is to act like you've already been working there. To arrive and start working and seem comfortable even if you aren't. Not cocky. Just comfortable-seeming. But I worried. I felt way too humble going into that dinner. I felt way too much like an interloper.

But I was no more of an interloper than they'd been. Everyone is when they start a new job. My inability to reconcile my current professional status with my lack of self-confidence wasn't crippling during my first day at work—after all, you can just hide away in your office or cube and type and pretend you're coming up with brilliant ideas. But at dinner, I felt stripped of all my defenses. I had to perform. I had to engage. I had to know who Werner Herzog is.

Werner fucking Herzog. I now know him to be a somewhat eccentric German director of strange and epic film sagas and esoteric documentaries. I am now a fan of both his work and the odd, intense prism through which he views odd and intense people. But that night it was just another cultural reference I didn't understand.

"Let's see what Ross thinks about Herzog," someone said. They weren't doing this maliciously—I know that now. I think they were doing it to include me because I wasn't talking, and they wanted me to talk. In any case, it was not what I wanted to hear.

There's a moment right after a person you respect engages you on something you do not understand when you have to decide if you are going to A. admit ignorance of the subject; B. point your tank toward a forest of bullshit and just barrel through; or C. answer with all-purpose responses much like the hard of hearing do.

I chose a combination of B and C.

"That guy. I think his early work was derivative. But his recent stuff has moved the needle."

Moved the needle? Moved . . . the needle? Movedthe-needle?

I had never used the expression "moved the needle" before that night, and I haven't since.

And so with that response, I lost them. I wasn't engaged in any meaningful way again the entire night. I sat there like a fourth grader who'd just moved to town and is starting his first day in the middle of the school year. I gave them no reason to think I was right for the job and no reason to think I was interesting to have around.

I should have said, "I have no idea who that is." **When we have no idea what's going on, we should always say, "I have no idea what you're talking about."** I love it when people enthusiastically admit ignorance. If a job candidate says, "I'm sorry. I have no idea what you're asking. Can you please explain?" during an interview, I consider that a positive— they seem honest, curious, and exacting. The problem wasn't that I didn't know a cultural reference; the problem was that I pretended that I did when I obviously didn't.

Knowing who those people around that table are now—many of them now my friends and cohorts—I cringe at my behavior. I was trying to play a part. I was trying to fit in. But they didn't need me to fit in. They needed me to be authentic. I was trying to apply the rules of business to the rules of dinner. But the workplace is not the same as a restaurant. We talk about things we don't understand all the time in business. To condemn bullshit at work would be to condemn the very foundations of enterprise. But bullshit doesn't work at dinner. They needed me to be an interesting conversationalist. They needed me to be an authentic human being. Being nervous and intimidated is fine. But you have to be authentic. **You cannot be an interesting conversationalist if you are faking interest in something.** It's not possible. If you don't know who Werner Herzog is, admit it. You will be compensated for the points you lose for ignorance with the points you gain for being conversationally fearless.

"I have no idea what you're talking about," you should say. Because you don't. And because you'd like to learn.

After the staff said good-bye I walked alone toward the C train to go home. A spitting rain seemed to mock me. After swiping my MetroCard at the turnstile a dozen or so times to try to get it to scan, I ran onto the train just as the doors closed.

I realized I was on the uptown train and not the downtown one just as the train pulled away from the station.

"This isn't going to work," I thought. "Six months, tops."

10

The Importance of Sucking at a New Job for a Year or Two

You suck.

Also: I suck.

I don't know what it is that you suck at, but you suck at something very important. You suck at things you will someday not suck at. But for now, you are not good at these things. In fact, you suck at them.

This must be accepted.

It might take a while. So I'll wait.

You know what? I'll do it too.

While we're both accepting that we suck, let's talk about failure.

Failure is huge right now. It's being studied. It's being written about. It's being blogged about. "Fail early and often," we're told. "Surrender to the pain of failure." "Failure is fundamental." The latest key to success is to fail but to fail in the right way.

But is there a right way to fail? Is there a right way to

submit work you know is half-baked, like I did during my first few months at *Esquire*? Is there a right way to stumble through a presentation to the sales staff, like I did during my first few months at *Esquire*? Is there a right way to indiscreetly talk about another magazine at a party and then turn around and two editors from that magazine are right behind you, like I did during my first few months at *Esquire*? Is there a right way to have a story killed? Is there a right way to do shit work?

I don't think actual failure is what's being discussed. "Failure" is just the word that makes the books and articles seem more intriguing than they actually are. Actual failure is awful and expensive. It's devastating. **Failure teaches you nothing. You should not consider "failure" a positive outcome. Not early. Not often. Not ever, if you can help it.** Really, what's being discussed is: mistakes.

All of the studies that the books and blog posts cite basically boil down to two messages. 1. Humans hate to make mistakes. 2. A key determinant of success is both accepting that you will make mistakes and paying attention to the mistakes that you make.

One of the most cited experts on this topic is Stanford psychologist Carol Dweck, who pioneered the idea of "mind-sets." People with "fixed mind-sets," she says, believe their abilities are unchangeable—a belief that causes them to shy away from situations in which they might fail. By contrast, people with "growth mind-sets" embrace challenges because they believe they can become smarter and more capable even if they don't succeed. They're willing to get things wrong, but more important, they're ready to listen to the feedback. Screwing up is not a defining thing. This is such a useful attitude to have. I've been at my current job for ten years and I've only just recently adopted this mentality. It's made my work better. It's made the process more efficient. And I have a lot more time to spend with my family.

What people with a growth mind set know is that mistakes are useful when you're willing to have a conversation about them, when you're willing to be corrected.

But actual failure? Humiliating, devastating failure?

Aside from teaching us that certain decisions are bad decisions and that we should not make them twice, failure totally blows. But mistakes are amazing.

The main failure of my first couple of years in New York was the shame I felt at making mistakes. If I have a regret, this is it. I was too caught up in the fear of making mistakes. I sometimes acted timidly. In the short term, I probably did "better" work, but in the long term I did worse work because I didn't allow myself to get my mistakes over with early. I would stay at work until midnight working on a headline. I would refine a single joke over two or three days. **There is nothing wrong with focusing on the details. But focusing on the details at the expense of your personal life is not a good idea.**

Now that I'm a manager, if I see someone hanging on to something for what I think is too long, I will tell them to give it to me. As is. Just turn it over. **Doing work too fast is a bad idea. But doing work too slow is a *terrible* idea.** The last thing a boss wants is to be left without any options if the work isn't good enough. **Being fastidious is possibly the worst thing a young worker can do.** The work is probably not going to get to where it needs to be no matter how long you hang on to it. So turn it in early and then make corrections. You're *supposed* to do bad work.

Everyone *wants* you to do bad work.

Everyone.

Your boss wants you to get it out of your system and learn what not to do.

And your peers want you to make mistakes too. Either they understand the value of a fearless colleague or they just want to feel superior . . . if they even notice. Loads of studies have shown that we tend to think people pay attention to us twice as much as they actually do. This is the spotlight effect. (Turns out my mom was right about this, which she repeated to me on a weekly basis during my adolescence.)

And you don't realize it, but *you* want to do bad work too. Because **in every bit of bad work, there is always a kernel of something good.** Bad work is 2 to 13 percent good. Your job is to pick through the mess you create and find that good. Other people will help you find it. Let them.

11

How to Smile

At some point during my first year at *Esquire*, I walked into the bar at the London Hotel on Fifty-Fourth Street where a bunch of my colleagues were hanging out in a banquette. I can't remember what the occasion was. Could've been a National Magazine Awards warm-up. Could've been the closing of a big issue. Could've been someone sent out an email with the question "Drink?" in the subject line.

I walked up to the gathering, and one of my fellow editors looked at me like he was Clint Eastwood in *For a Few Dollars More* and uttered six words that forever changed my general bearing in the workplace.

"Why are you so fucking glum?"

Now, I am not what you'd call a good-time Charlie. I am not jaunty, chirpy, or cheery. I am not one to spread sunshine anywhere, much less all over the place. My resting face is vaguely troubled. I don't smile a lot is the point.

And I smiled hardly at all my first couple of years in New York—almost certainly due to stress and feeling in over my head.

But I wasn't aware of this until that night at the London Hotel bar.

My colleague had clearly been offended for a while and had finally had just enough alcohol to let that offense be known. The reason for his offense is because a frown is demoralizing. And it's contagious. But, helpfully, so is smiling. Science says so.

Here's a fun activity: Smile.

No, really . . . *smile.*

Look, this isn't fun for me either.

We're not moving ahead here until I get a simper.

Since you're responding to instruction and not something that actually makes you happy, the smile on your face is probably *not* what the psychologists call a "true" smile or a "Duchenne" smile, after the pioneering nineteenth-century French neurologist. The smile on your face is soulless. When you don't like the way you look in a photo, it's probably because you're smiling this way. What's happening is you're contracting the zygomaticus major, which pulls up the corners of your mouth, but you're not involving the orbicularis oculi, the muscles that cause the corners of your eyes to crinkle. The orbicularis oculi are very difficult to contract voluntarily. You almost always need to be actually delighted in order for them to engage.

So think of something that delights you. A child with a balloon. If you don't like children, maybe just a balloon. If you don't like balloons, then you are dead inside, and the smile is the least of your problems.

Anyway, find your joy.

(Note: That will be the last time I ever type "find your joy"—in this book or in any other media, known or unknown, throughout the universe, in perpetuity.)

Now, that's a genuine smile. That's what makes you photogenic. That's what makes you "light up."

That smile on your face is a powerful tool. The Germans confirmed it in a now-classic study. Researchers had people look at *The Far Side* cartoons while either holding a pen in their teeth (forcing a "smile") or pressing it between their lips. The former group found the cartoons funnier than did the latter—suggesting they were more easily delighted because they'd already been "smiling." It's like magic, really. Smiling begets happiness, which begets smiling, and so on.

If this doesn't come naturally, just **smile 20 percent wider than feels comfortable.** You want to give it the ol' Julia Roberts. Try squinting slightly, which will involve the muscles around the eyes. You want to feel like George Clooney looks. Remember: **If you're not feeling a little**

stupid, then the smile's not working. Though you might feel awkward, you won't look awkward. You'll look satisfied and confident and happy to be there. Everyone's better off— especially you. And all you had to do was be happy.

And feel stupid.

But mainly: be happy.

12

How to Shut Up

At *Esquire,* there is a production meeting each week where the editors and designers are supposed to discuss the status of projects. The point of the meeting is to have a weekly milepost where you know you will have to answer for your work. Your answers should mostly be "Yes" and "Wednesday" and "Looking good." I did not understand this my first few months at *Esquire.* I thought I was supposed to *answer questions truthfully and expansively.* So in response to "How's that story coming?" I would explain and apologize and answer questions that hadn't been asked. I would bore everyone in the room. I didn't know I was supposed to say, "It's great," and then I was supposed to shut up.

This is how to talk in a meeting.

1. Shh.
2. Shh.

3. Speak.

4. Shh.

If you have already opened your mouth, then by all means please finish your sentence, and then: Just stop talking. Stop. You're talking and talking and you think this is how you're going to prove your worth to your colleagues. But it isn't. You're not letting other people speak and you're creating chances for you to make a fool out of yourself. **In meetings—in regular weekly staff meetings especially— you prove your worth through discretion, not action, by saying just what it is you know, and by saying it clearly and concisely and then shutting up.**

"How's that coming?"

"It's great."

Done. Everybody's happy. Now the meeting can move on.

Now, if it's not great, you will pay a price for bullshitting everyone. You will be found out later on, and that will be a problem. So say it's great only if it's actually great or "fine" or even "moving right along." (In the workplace, "great" is a linguistic chameleon.)

The key here is: Make sure it is great. Then you have nothing to worry about.

Here is what not to do, ever.

How's that project coming?

"Well . . ."

Never start off a sentence with "Well." Leave "well" to the airline pilots ("Well, folks, we just heard from the tower, and it's a total shit show"). Nothing good has ever come after the word "well."

". . . I met with . . ."

No one cares who you met with.

". . . the team . . ."

Oy, with "the team."

". . . and we determined . . ."

Dear god, nobody cares. I'm getting bored typing this.

Maybe that's what the meeting is about: you, the team, what you discussed with the team, how the team's doing, the team's dreams. Boy, what a wonderful team! **Here's the test: Are you interested in what you're saying? If not, then stop saying it.** Just stop talking. Midsentence if you have to.

Discretion is a virtue. The most underrated tactic in the workplace is silence.

13

Things You Should Never Say in a Professional Setting

I am sometimes told—usually by magazine designers who are waiting on a decision from me—that I am overthinking things. "I think you're overthinking this," they say. Despite the fact that they may very well be correct, I would like to ban "I think you're overthinking this" from the canon of common workplace expressions. It punishes people for caring, for trying to make something great. I think that people who accuse other people of overthinking just don't feel like thinking. Which is thoughtless.

Here are a few other things it's unwise to say in a professional setting.

"I'm sorry."

You can say, "I understand this was wrong, and it won't happen again." You can explain what happened if asked. But consider leaving the apologies to your personal life. Apologies are purely emotional.

Acknowledging the problem and saying how you will correct it is a lot more professionally valuable.

"...Does that make any sense?"

People like to ask this after making a point. If you have to ask this, then you either are not confident in what you just said or you don't know what you just said and you are now asking the person listening to your nonsense to validate it.

"It is what it is."

Yes, but what is it? If you take this idea to its natural conclusion you will end up smoking a cigarette while jumping off a cliff. We must all resolve to stop saying this. It means nothing. It is a mantra for idiots.

"Everything happens for a reason."

See: "It is what it is."

"Let's grab a coffee."

Let's grab a coffee. Let's grab a lunch. Can I grab you for five minutes? *Can you grab me for five minutes?* I mean, that depends on what you're grabbing, you know? And will you be grabbing me for the full five minutes or just at the beginning? May I grab you, too? Grabbing is an aggressive thing.

And it suggests that the person making the request for your time doesn't think you're worth a full, focused experience or that they aren't. It's noncommittal. We should *have*, not grab. Have lunch. Have a meeting. Have some coffee.

"I had this dream last night."

Let me guess: We were both in it—it was like we were at work but it wasn't really work and there was this little man, not a dwarf really, but just, like, a little guy, and he was holding this cake and on the cake said . . . well, I forget what it said. . . . But Taylor Swift was there. . . . The recounting of dreams ranks as the third most boring thing to talk about behind the new JavaScript update and a really bad hangover. Speaking of . . .

"I'm so hungover . . ."

No one wants to hear about your hangover. No one. You don't even want to hear about your hangover.

"I feel . . ."

You may think at work. But you may not feel.

"Stop telling me I'm overthinking this."

Because you probably are.

14

How to Have a Meaningful Lunch in a Fancy Restaurant Full of Important People

My first lunch at the Four Seasons on East Fifty-Second Street in Midtown Manhattan was to celebrate my first anniversary at *Esquire.* Just me and the boss.

The Four Seasons is *the* old-school restaurant for old-school important lunches when you are involved in old-school media. It is stuffy. It serves pretty good food. There's gold stuff hanging from the ceiling. It's got everything important people need to have lunch.

The layout is peculiar: You have a long row of bench seating with seats facing out toward the tables in the center of the restaurant, which is shaped like a rectangle. There are tables in the center. Then there's a balcony with tables overlooking the tables in the center. So you have important people on the benches staring out at important people in the middle, all overlooked by important people up on the balcony.

After we sat down at one of the bench tables, I noticed

Lou Dobbs and Jack Cafferty, both with CNN at the time, sitting next to us. Interesting thing about the bench seating: Everybody faces the same direction. Imagine Lou Dobbs and Jack Cafferty sitting in a pickup truck, staring out at a bunch of cattle. That's exactly what they look like eating at the Four Seasons. That's what my boss and I looked like. That's pretty much what everyone looks like. You have one eye on your companion. And one eye on everyone else.

The problem with the important lunch (especially the first-anniversary lunch) is: You don't know what the rules are. Do you start talking about business immediately? After all, this is a business lunch. Do you talk about your personal life as you typically do during meals? But this is a business lunch. Do you point out the fact that that's Martha Stewart over there? Do you ask if you think that stuff hanging from the ceilings is real gold? Are we drinking or what? (Did I say that out loud?)

I'm here to tell you after having been to a lot of these: The business lunch is a date, interrupted at some point by earnestness. You schmooze for a little while, order the food, schmooze, eat the food, then talk business. Which begs the question: Why not just go have a drink? Or meet on a park bench for fifteen minutes? Do we really want to look at our colleagues and business associates eating food? Do we really want to commit to the time it takes to eat a meal? In any case, after years of observations and in-the-field experience, here is a field guide to the business lunch.

"WE DRINKING?": If the waiter asks what you would like to drink first, and you would like to drink, but only if the important person you're with plans to drink, then order a club soda. Club soda is basically fun water. And the fun of club soda is an indication to the other person that you'd likely have a drink should the other person order one. That club soda is a solid complement to any alcoholic beverage means you can just add to your drink order should your companion end up drinking, rather than replace the drink order.

Occasionally someone will suggest wine for the table. Or drinks. If you don't want to drink, don't drink. If this seems to offend or bewilder the person you're having lunch with, this is a clue that they're unreasonable and pushy, which is a bigger problem than this whole drinking situation. So you say, unapologetically: "I'm not drinking." No hemming. No hawing. No excuses. No apologies. No hostility. "I'm not drinking."

PEOPLE COMING OVER TO SAY HELLO: Do not be alarmed by the number of people who will come over and say hello to your important companion. These people will stroll over to your table and smile and spew out small talk and laugh at things that aren't funny. What this is, is success-onset personality disorder (SOPD), and it afflicts 90 percent of the rich and powerful. The behavior of SOPD sufferers is marked by a discrepancy between what is actually being said and the emotional response to it. Also, you will understand none of the references they make. The drop-by will go something like this . . .

Your companion: Hey there, [Person Slightly Less Important Than the Important Person You're Dining With]!

[Important Person Who Would Not Agree That He Is Less Important]: Looking well, I see! Ha-ha-ha-ha.

Your companion: Yes! Ha-ha-ha-ha.

[The Slightly Less Important Person looks over to you by doing the thing where you turn to the other person while keeping your eyes closed; then you open them.]: Hi, I'm [Slightly Less Important Person].

You: Nice to meet you.

[Reverse closed-eye pivot back over to the important person.]

Slightly Less Important Person: How's [add nickname of person you don't know, like Strap or something]?

Your companion: Oh, she's hangin' in there. You still get up to [NAME OF PLACE IN THE HAMP-TONS OR SOMETHING] in the summer?

Slightly Less Important Person: No, we're doing [OTHER PLACE IN THE HAMPTONS, PROBABLY] now.

Your companion: *I* hear it's nice. The sunsets. Ha-ha-ha-ha.

Slightly Less Important Person: Well, good seeing you. I need to get back to [some dude over there checking his phone].

MISLEADING FOOD: There will be a menu item that is mis-leadingly named.

Sir, I just want to make sure you know the salmon burger is a pudding made from salmon roe and the salad is a sprinkling of endive powder.

FRUIT SOUP: **Important people seem to like fruit soup.** Which is a smoothie poured into a bowl and then called "fruit soup."

WHEN TO BRING UP BUSINESS MATTERS: If you have something you want to say to the important person you are having lunch with, do not wait until the end of the meal to say it. But wait long enough for the food to come. **The serious stuff at a business lunch should be discussed between the entrée and dessert, which is the longest stretch of time you're not interrupted by a waiter.** Conversation with your companion during the important lunch goes something like this:

Bullshit.

Bullshit.

Bullshit.

Substance.

Bullshit.

Awkward eye contact with Lou Dobbs.

Bullshit.

Check, please.

If you have something to talk about. If you're unhappy about something. If you want to take on new responsibility. If you want to open up some avenue of discussion, do it now. This is your best chance. The other person is captive and possibly a little tipsy. Now is the time.

THE CHECK: If you are a client of the other person, you are probably not getting the check, but you should make the move.

If you are professional acquaintances with similar social standing, the check will be paid by whoever made the invitation. But the other person should make the move.

If you're eating with your boss to celebrate your first anniversary you're obviously not getting the check and the hesitant move we make where we reach toward our money is a silly thing to do. You both know who's getting this one. If you do make this move, your boss will look at you like you're crazy. (Trust me.)

15

A Few More Rules for the Business Lunch

Reservations. Always. Even for that place where you know they can seat you.

If you're a party of two at a four-top, sit next to each other, not across from each other. At a business lunch, intimacy is a virtue. There might be secrets. Now, I know that if you are used to always sitting across from your companion this will seem strangely . . . close. But you'll see its benefits immediately. Anyway, do you really want to stare at the other person while he's eating? Do you want to be stared at?

No red sauce.

No burgers.

No burgers involving a red sauce.

Nothing else that is typically eaten with your hands: burritos, burgers, ribs, tacos, sandwiches.

You want to have soup? Have soup.

You want to spoon the broth toward you and not away

from you, in defiance of various soup-eating etiquette sources? Have at it.

Nothing described as "scratch-made." Takes too long.

No osso buco or lasagna. Takes too long.

Notorious tooth magnets: spinach, broccoli, poppy seeds, blackberries.

Nothing that might squirt when pierced. Ravioli, baked tomato, lobster, dumplings.

Note: If your food has squirted you, a lemon slice works wonders.

Spend no more than twenty seconds deciding what to order. Just look at the menu. Order that thing that seems vaguely appealing.

If there's a lot more food on your plate than on everyone else's plate, you are talking too much.

If you're done before everyone else, you need to talk more.

Consider forgoing dessert.

And ask for the check with the coffee.

Finally, ignore any of the above guidelines if implementing them would make you uncomfortable. Order what you want, drink what you want. (Note: One drink will improve the work you do after lunch. Two drinks will damage it. Three drinks will ensure that it won't get done.) But do everything efficiently, so that the mechanics of lunch don't get in the way of the point of it, which is to have an interesting conversation with interesting people.

16

How to Make Small Talk

I am not a good small talker. And I had to do a lot of small talk my first years in New York. Everyone I met was a stranger. Every party I attended was a room full of people I didn't know.

I met lots of people whose work I already admired—writers, actors—but attempting to talk to them was brutal. It wasn't that I didn't speak; it's that I would say weird things.

"You were tremendous in *A Serious Man*."
Oscar-nominated-but-not-a-household-name actor:
"I wasn't in that."
"Ah."

I'm just not good at it. I'm still not, but after having been in a lot of small-talk situations over the past ten years, I am better at it. Or at least I better understand it.

The first thing to acknowledge in a small-talk situation is that we live in a society. And as someone who lives in a society, you have entered into a mutual agreement to speak when it would be awkward not to. That agreement has afforded us great things—such as knowing whether or not you'll need an umbrella when you get outside and also . . . you know . . . civilization. People who don't speak when close together are really no different from penguins on an expanse of ice, huddled together being mostly silent. And where are the penguins anyway? Yes, they're somehow noble and adorable at the same time and their adventures are worthy of a Morgan Freeman narration, but are their social mores really *working* for them?

Consider a 2014 study of commuters by some University of Chicago psychologists. In one experiment, train riders were asked to strike up a conversation with a stranger on their morning commute, sit alone quietly, or just do as they normally did. Afterward, the chatty group reported having the more enjoyable ride. In another experiment, a survey of commuters showed that while they were interested in talking to others, they believed others didn't want to talk to them nearly as much. Taken together, it points toward something called "pluralistic ignorance"—we go along with what's happening in a social situation because we wrongly believe everyone else wants it that way. It's why we pass someone on the street even though they look like they need help. And it's why we don't talk on elevators even though we like connecting with others. What the results of the study suggest is that we don't speak with strangers *despite* the fact that we actually want to. If any one idea should guide your professional social interactions, let it be this one.

The second thing is: **If you're not curious, the small talk is not going to work. So get curious.** Obviously you must maintain eye contact and smile. Which suggest curiosity. Remark on something that is clearly interesting but not intimately personal, such as the large box that guy is holding or that weird sound coming from the other room. Reveal something about yourself. And *listen.* It's amazing to me how little I used to listen to people when they were talking. Now when I make a conscious effort to listen, it's as if I've turned up the volume or put in a hearing aid or acquired a soul. Listening is a tool. When you listen, you access a new dimension of the conversation. That kind of presence is helpful in small talk. It gives you access to nuances that can cue new and interesting points of conversation. And what it leads to is: *medium talk.*

Medium talk occurs when people's souls connect with their professional selves. It can happen on the floor of a convention, in a meeting room, anywhere. All you need to spark is a flash of humanity. Medium talk is about observations, not reports; how someone's vacation actually was, not "How's your vacation? Good, I hope. Anyway, about the P-32 delivery. . . . "; ideas, not things.

(Note: Large talk is not advisable. You go large, and all of a sudden you're talking about the Crimean separatists and a regrettable relationship in the '90s. Which is heading toward huge talk and is a little too sizable for a professional situation.)

17

A List of Small-Talk Topics for People Who Hate Small Talk

Small dogs. Affenpinschers, say. Maltese. Silky terriers.

The weather in some location other than where you find yourself currently.

"What are your hopes for _____?" (Could be for something they're working on, could be for the rest of the evening.)

"Why did you choose that drink?" (This will inevitably lead to something interesting. For a story on drinking in bars, I once assigned a writer/cocktail waitress to ask customers why they chose to order what they chose to order. What you learn is: The drink always corresponds to the overall mood of the day someone has had and that people really like talking about the day they've had.)

The origins of the other person's last name.

Some deficiency of yours. (Your ignorance of what makes a good passed food, say.)

The fact that basically all male fashion design has been derived from hunting or military dress. (It's true.)

The design quality of this ballroom carpet.

How, if you put salt on your coaster, the drink won't stick to it. (It's true.)

A compliment.

A planned vacation.

Penguins.

I mean, they just stand around!

Small talk itself.

18

How to Have a Short but Meaningful Conversation in an Elevator

The elevators in the building that house magazine staffs are uniquely entertaining places to be. Media people are verbally bipolar. When we're not being guarded and insecure, we tend to be, how do you say, expressive. There can be a lot of talking. And then the talking often moves into an area that clearly demands discretion. But instead of pausing the conversation until privacy can be gotten, they just whisper.

"SO DID YOU TALK TO HIM?"

"OH YEAH."

"WELL."

"WELL, HERE'S THE THING. He was, like, "Look I don't know where I'm at right now in my life. I'm still reeling from the breakup." And then he was, like, "You're kind of clingy." CAN YOU BELIEVE THAT?!"

That kind of thing stresses me out. Even the prospect of it stresses me out.

For me, waiting for an elevator makes me feel like I'm Atreyu approaching the Southern Oracle in *The NeverEnding Story.*

Right?

For those readers who weren't in elementary school in the mid-eighties, *The NeverEnding Story* is a 1984 fantasy movie about a boy named Atreyu on a quest to defeat the Nothing. Along the way, he approaches the Southern Oracle, via a passage guarded by two colossal crouching figures with claws, wings, and eyes that shoot deadly lasers. This is how I feel when approaching any social situation— but especially elevators.

When will the doors open? Who will be inside the elevator? Will I feel compelled to talk with that person? Will someone come along and wait with me? Will I need to talk with *that* person? Will that person be my boss? Will that be weird?

And when I get *in* the elevator, will I be engaged to make small talk? And how will I manage that? And why is Larry standing alone in the *middle* of the elevator? Who does that?

Hey, man!
Hey, Larry.
Weekend plans?
Not really.

At least it's Friday, right?
It's Thursday.

So it's just like *The NeverEnding Story*, only instead of a pair of giant, winged, strangely alluring half-woman/half-lioness creatures who kill men with their eye lasers, it's a dude wearing Crocs and an amiable demeanor.

But here's the thing: I'm the one making this fraught, not Larry. Larry is hopeful. Larry is social. Larry knows something that I have a hard time fully embracing:

An elevator is a prison of opportunity.

It's an opportunity to offer a compliment, to make an innocuous comment, to acknowledge that you have something in common with whomever you're standing next to—even if it's only to remark on the weather. **(The weather is not a boring topic for small talk. Nothing else affects every single person in your general area in exactly the same way at exactly the same time. It is our common ground. For conversation, weather is a gift.)**

If you're at work and you end up on the elevator with someone you know, the opportunity demands small talk. About anything but work.

(Let's all resolve never to say "I got your email" on an elevator.)

You have to look at everyone on the elevator as people on a journey rather than humans being conveyed. This works for any small-talk situation. Everyone is just here on their way to something more interesting.

But if you can make *this* interesting—if you can make this human and meaningful? This time before the meeting starts, this stupid drinks thing at the convention, this elevator ride?

Now we're getting somewhere.

19

How to Pitch Something

My job involves a lot of pitching. I am sometimes the pitch*ee*. I am sometimes the pitch*er*. I frequently alternate between the two roles in the same professional relationship. I can call up a publicity rep one day and make a pitch that my magazine is where her client should do her next big interview and be told no. *Pitcher.* Two months later I might get a call from that same publicity rep who tells me that now is the time for her client to do an interview in my magazine. *Pitchee.*

There is very little bullshit that goes on with these discussions, even if the rep and I might not know each other very well. That's because the stakes and the score are clear. The advantages and disadvantages of their client being associated with my magazine are clear. All they want to know is: How many pages? Will there be a photo shoot? In person or on the phone? Time commitment? And when's it being published? I could be a raging asshole, and if those terms work, they will probably say yes.

They'll say yes because my offer fits into their agenda. The other person's agenda is an underrated thing. You're not in charge. The agenda is.

Advice on pitching usually involves the tenor of it instead of the content of it. Know your audience; map out your pitch in advance; practice, practice, practice; anticipate criticisms, keep your answers to questions brief, and then pivot back to your message. All solid advice, but even if it's the best pitch that's ever been pitched, if the idea doesn't mesh with the pitchee's agenda, then it's not going to happen.

This is the first of three factors that should decrease your anxiety.

The second is the fact that you actually believe in what you're pitching.

. . .

What do you mean you're not sure you believe in what you're pitching? Of course you believe. Your idea will change everything. It will win awards. It will change lives.

Obviously.

(Note: If I have not convinced you that you actually believe in your idea, then you have bigger problems than the pitch. So, my suggestion is: Go find something to believe in. Your career is too short for limp pitches.)

*   *   *

Here's how to pitch an idea you believe in:

Talk.

Talk. Now, if you, like me, are not what people typically describe as "dripping with gusto," then you have to raise your game a little. I know. For those of us who are wry and dry, this feels like a betrayal of our souls. But it is not. Because you aren't the most important thing here. Your idea is. So get "up." I'm not talking about passion per se. But I am talking about fervor.

Because you *believe.*

Amen?

Amen.

(Hallelujah.)

For my column in *Entrepreneur* magazine, I frequently use venture capitalists as sources. And the advice they typically give to entrepreneurs pitching them is: 1. Point out the problem. 2. Offer a solution. 3. Say why your solution is better than all other solutions. 4. Say why you (or whoever you're representing) have been working so long to make this solution happen.

The pitch is the middle of a long story. The beginning is everything that's led up to this moment. The end of the story is what will happen after the idea is accepted. The pitch itself is a key part of the story. Your audience is a part of the story.

Here's a test for determining if you have a solid pitch.

Look into the mirror and pitch yourself.

(Note: Looking into a mirror is not necessary. In fact, don't look into the mirror.)

As you're pitching, ask yourself one crucial question: Are you bored? Because if you're bored, then whoever you're pitching to is going to be *really* bored. And if you're bored, you're probably bored because you've buried the point. The core pitch should be about fifteen seconds long. An old cliché states that you should be able to pitch any idea over the course of a single elevator ride. This is true. Even if you're going only one floor up.

Here's the third thing that will decrease your anxiety and make you better at pitching: **Everyone in the room wants you to succeed.** They want to be using their time to listen to a great idea. Which means you immediately know if it's not working. You either get nothing or you get something. If your pitch doesn't work, you'll know. Because the bar is so low and because everyone wants you to deliver a good pitch, if you get nothing and you have nothing else to give, then it's over. If it's being received well, of course, you'll get some sort of positive reaction, even if it's only a raised eyebrow or a nod of a head.

A successful pitch requires belief, brevity, and enough enthusiasm to pique interest but not so much that you turn that interest into concern for your emotional well-being. If you believe in what you're saying, then the rest is easy. Because if you believe—like, really believe— then all you have to do is talk.

20

A Few Words on Passion

One of the commonly accepted virtues of business in the twenty-first century—especially for people who commonly have to pitch ideas—is: passion.

Intensity I get. But passion?

There are those of us who don't respond well to extreme passion. We're the skeptics. And we've always annoyed the zealots: "Why won't they just listen?!" the zealots say. Well, frankly, the passion is making it hard to listen. The problem with passion is that it can cloud your message and overshadow your mission enough that it's no longer clear what you're pitching.

It's one thing to throw out an idea during a meeting. It's another to say, "All right, guys. Listen to this! Here's what we're gonna do. We're gonna . . ."

You end up sounding like Mickey Rooney rallying a bunch of teenagers to "put on a show" and raise 280 bucks to save an orphanage.

The more passionate you are, the less professional you seem—the less human you seem. At some point, passion begins to mask the humanity it seeks to express.

But there's a way to be passionate without seeming crazy. It involves what absolutely no expert refers to as the "enthuse, temper, enthuse" approach, or ETE. The idea is to occasionally, and quite explicitly, undercut your passion with self-deprecation or even hedging. When you're talking passionately about your product, idea, or business, you need to tone down the enthusiasm, so that it's obvious to your audience that you aren't on some one-track mission to convince everyone of your own brilliance. On the highway of enthusiasm, you need to stop every now and then and stretch your legs, take a restroom break, buy some beef jerky. You need to relax and look around. By acknowledging— even vaguely—that your idea is not The Great Idea but one in a cosmos of good ideas, you're making your notion even more appealing. You're placing it in a sane context—the context of the rigor that it will take to get the idea off the ground.

21

How to Shake a Hand (Feat. Kanye West)

The best shaker of hands I've ever encountered was Kanye West, July 2011 at the Nassau Coliseum on Long Island, backstage at a Rihanna concert. I was introduced to him, and he shook my hand, saying, "I'm Kanye. I like your magazine."

A deconstruction of this interaction:

[West extends a hand] "I'm Kanye." [begins shake] "I" [pump] "like" [pump] "your" [pump] "magazine" [pump].

Note that despite the information conveyed, the elapsed time was approximately one second.

Ilikeyourmagazine. Pumppumppumppump.

[Henceforth, the handshake with synchronized compliment shall be known as the Westian Pump.]

Even with greetings, Kanye has flow.

The worst handshake of my life was with a motivational speaker. Although I try to keep my interactions with people in the business of inspiration to a minimum (many motivational speakers are preachers without the benefit of being backed by a choir), journalism affords you a lot of opportunities to shake hands with unlikely people and so there I was having my hand shaken by a man typical of his ilk: off-puttingly buoyant and overly familiar. His grip was firm enough, but he just kept shaking my hand. As he looked at me, he told me what my name was, presumably so he could commit it to memory. Twice. And then he kept shaking my hand. This is a classic motivational speaker move: In an attempt to create a meaningful connection, they overstep and make the connection meaningful in the worst possible way. (**Rule: In an intimate setting, motivational speakers are always demoralizing.**) Shaking a hand for too long is the kind of thing you do if you're trying to hold someone in place so an assassin can line up an easy shot. It's emotionally uncomfortable and an awful way to start a relationship.

Kanye West, a man who has developed a reputation as a megalomaniacal blowhard, introduced himself with grace, deference, and efficiency. Yet the passion merchant, whose job it is to inspire people, introduced himself with smarm and a deliberateness that bordered on lethargy. When I hear that Kanye West has once again gotten flack for saying something like, "For me to say I wasn't a genius, I would just be lying to you and to myself," or "I am a god. Now what?" or "I'm fighting with the way I line my words up together and the way I place a sweater on top of a T-shirt," my reaction is always: Yes, but the man can shake a hand.

The handshake is inherently weird, of course. Holding a stranger's hand, creating a human joint, and then rhythmically moving that joint up and down? That is weird. But its weirdness is what makes it such an opportunity, what makes it crucial.

And a little fraught.

There are three ways to screw up a handshake.

The first way is to hold it too long. This tends to occur with motivational speakers and the lonely.

The second way is to squeeze too much. This is the least offensive bad way to shake a hand. With the handshake you want to err on the side of injuring people.

The third way is to be too dainty. To the dainty shakers, the rest of us ask you: Why? The light grip and single pump suggest tentativeness, which is a cardinal sin in business, especially when you're meeting someone for the first time. There are a handful of people in my professional life who give me the ol' May-I-Have-This-Waltz-Why-No-You-May-Not whenever I see them. It feels like they must have something to hide. All other aspects of their comportment suggest they're on the up-and-up, yet the sickeningly limp handshake leaves room for doubt.

(There used to be a fourth way: The Palm Tickler. But

it mostly died out in the 1970s, along with prog rock and Groucho Marx.)

Obviously, the handshake should be firm, but not too firm. It should last about a second. It should involve three or four rapid pumps, and eye contact and a smile for the duration. This is not a mystery. The handshake is simple.

A word on "firm": With handshakes, the key part of your anatomy is not the palm, but the weblike area between the thumb and forefinger. That's the adductor pollicis muscle. The way to firmly shake a hand is to perform a meeting of your adductor pollicis muscle with the other person's adductor pollicis muscle. In sexual terms you want to perform a kind of "scissoring" involving that area. You want to "get up in there." You want to rock the other adductor pollicis's world. But only for about a second.

It's been studied, it turns out.

In 2008, a group of researchers led by a University of Iowa business professor had five different people shake the hand of each participant in a mock job interview. Specifically, they had to "close their hand around the participant's hand but wait for the participant to initiate the strength of the grip and the upward-and-down shaking [and to] release their grip only when the participant began to relax his or her grip." Then they were asked to rate each handshake on five dimensions: "completeness of grip, strength, duration, vigor, and eye contact."

Those ratings were then compared with the hiring recommendations made by a separate group of mock interviewers. The result: Participants who scored big on handshaking—a firm, complete grip with good eye contact and enthusiastic up-and-down motion—were also judged the most hireable.

A handshake represents us and it makes promises. It's the most physically intimate thing we do in business. It says that you're ready to join forces in a metaphorical way because you have, for a couple of seconds at least, joined forces in a physical way. So if you're going to shake a hand, then shake a hand. Be firm but not too firm. Be vigorous but not too vigorous. Look the other person in the eyes. Maybe throw in a little love like Kanye while you're at it. And hold it for long enough that it seems meaningful, but not so long that it seems comical. Or painful. Or even worse: weird.

22

How to Be Late

One thing that I love about New York is that people seem to be on time here more than in other places. Meetings tend to start on time. People are slightly early to lunches. I'm not sure why. After all, there are a lot of obstacles that can get in your way: A broken-down subway train. A cabbie who tells you to get out of his cab when you suggest that maybe driving through Times Square isn't the best idea. A parade. But these things are so common that people seem to allow time for them. New Yorkers are rarely late.

I have been late to fewer than twenty events in my life. (I can tell you exactly because they've been recorded in *The Tiny Book of Blunders*, a small leather-bound journal I keep in my desk drawer.)

Seven of those instances involved crosstown Midtown traffic, which, in my defense, is an utterly unknowable factor. To predict it is to deny that the hansom cab still exists here as some kind of Brigadoon-like fantasy; that the president of the United States sometimes comes to the Midtown Grand Hyatt to give a speech and when he wants to drive a couple of blocks to the UN all of Midtown must stop moving for twenty minutes; and that that UPS driver is just gonna park in the middle of a street, deliver a package, and then just, you know, shoot the shit with the DOORMAN WHAT THE HELL?!

Ten of those instances involved making a moral decision whereby I decided my time was better used changing someone's flat tire or stanching someone's bleeding.

And the others I have blocked out entirely because they're too painful.

For me, earliness is not a condition but a state.

Being late is arguably a better way to live your life. You're never alone in a room. You don't get stuck making as much small talk. You seem like you have an interesting life since all of its events just seem to *smash together.* And you never have to eat the shitty appetizers at a party because the early people will have already reckoned with them and warned you in advance.

Because I've been witness to perhaps five hundred thousand instances of other people being late—give or take—and because I consider myself morally superior to habitually late people, I've developed some guidelines for how best to go about it:

Don't explain why you're late. If you don't explain

that you overslept, there still exists the possibility that you've spent the last thirty minutes cradling an injured bird in your hands. Also: On the hierarchy of things no one cares about, "reason for being late" falls in between "your dream last night" and "how adorable your three-year-old niece is."

If you're late to a meeting, don't ask a question or make a point for ten minutes after you arrive. Because it's probably already been covered.

Don't ask, "What'd I miss?"

In a morning meeting, don't do the thing where you take the lid off the coffee and then hold it with both hands and then move it close to your nose so you can relish its aroma for a little bit and then oops there's some foam on your nose!

Oh, now you're yawning.

Now you're *audibly* yawning.

Aw, you're just waking up, you sleepyhead!

If you're late to an *interview*, don't make an excuse. Just be frank and remorseful. You must acknowledge how mortified you are. And you must say what actually happened—be it sleeping late or traffic or you just generally screwed up. Authenticity and candor are important professional virtues and that's the kind of thing we like around here and we just have a feeling about you, when can you start?!

Don't make a habit of it.

Or, if you do make a habit of it, just make sure that you're really, really good. Here are your options: *punctual and talented* (you'll do great things), *late and talented* (you'll be OK), *punctual and mediocre* (you'll be OK), *late and mediocre* (you're screwed).

23

How to Be on Time, for Chrissakes

Time management is never about managing time. Time is a known and stable factor, after all. It doesn't change. What it was last year, it will be this year. It can't be managed—it can only be acknowledged or ignored. And cursed while you're showering. But that won't change it.

If you're late for a meeting, it's probably not because some unavoidable obstacle put itself in your way. It's because you didn't allow for the obstacle. You didn't spend time anticipating the obstacle. And if you didn't spend time anticipating the obstacle, you're not respecting the people you're doing business with. In other words, *you* are the obstacle. **If you want to be on time, you will be on time. Because being on time is easy. Respecting time is the tricky part.**

There are many opportunities to be late or on time, but for the purposes of this chapter, let's stick with the most useful example: the meeting.

For the first time ever, I am about to reveal how to be on time for a meeting. Countless studies by scientists, the military, various government agencies, and the inventor of Clocky, "the alarm clock that runs away," have all come together to prove that the way to be on time for a meeting is as follows:

Be on time for the meeting.

There is no skill. There is nothing to learn.

Because if you want to be on time, you'll be on time. People who are consistently late make lots of excuses: traffic, children, illness, inclement weather, "They mixed up my macchiato with someone's misto," etcetera. But those excuses are representative of one thing: A disregard for what you're supposed to be on time for. Whatever the meeting is about, it's just not important enough.

After all, we're on time all the time. We tend to eat on time. We press the gas when the light is green. We say hello immediately after someone else says hi. So when we decide *not* to be on time—and it is always a decision—the message isn't "I'm too busy." The message is "I don't respect this enough to do the easiest thing in the world: just show up."

Being late is about a ton of little decisions you make on the way to being late. It's never just about the moment in time when you're scheduled to meet. It's about days of preparation. Months, even. In some ways, years. Because an inability to keep an appointment is about something much larger than the hour at hand. If you're struggling with being on time, imagine that your meeting is a lot more important than it actually is. Imagine that your being late would scuttle the whole thing. Imagine the meeting is, oh, I don't know, a rocket launch. Launch day is just launch day. The launch *campaign* is the thing that gets the rocket launched.

You are NASA. Your schedule is filled with rocket launches. For god's sake, get those sons of bitches off the ground on time.

24

How to Find a Good Bar to Drink in After Work

For the first two years I worked at *Esquire,* three or four times a week I walked over to the key-shaped red marble bar at San Domenico, an Italian restaurant just off New York City's Columbus Circle on Central Park South and the closest good bar near the office. My companion was usually David "Curc" Curcurito, *Esquire*'s design director, who started at the magazine only a few months before me. I drank Oban, a fourteen-year-old single-malt Scotch, because that's what Curc drank. I was not what you'd call a sophisticated drinker. He could've ordered a Frangelico spritzer and I would've said, "Make it two."

We drank a lot. I'm not just referring to drinking *over time.* I mean that when we drank, we drank a lot because San Domenico had Renato, the best bartender who ever worked in New York City. Three reasons: 1. Nobody looks better in a red double-breasted sport coat with gold buttons than Renato. And 2. Every time we'd turn around to look out the window toward Central Park and turn back around we'd find our glasses full. It was beautiful. And 3. He rarely spoke but when he did, he always said exactly the right thing. So we drank there a lot. San Domenico quickly became our place.

A place is very useful. It's a satellite office, really. It should be no more than five minutes away from your workplace. Otherwise you won't go frequently enough to establish a rhythm. If after drinking there for the first time you decide this could be your place, you have to go back once within the next five days. And then at least twice a week thereafter. (No one said this was going to be easy.)

The bar should have a name that you're not embarrassed to say out loud. Bars with names that are plural forms of common nouns are not desirable: For example, "Meet me at Whispers" is not an invitation that can be taken seriously—by a business associate or anyone else.

The bartender should buy you a drink every once in a while. If that's not happening, even if everything else is going smoothly, you don't have a place.

Also: The best bartenders are vaguely disinterested. Bartenders who aren't all that communicative seem to be better at keeping your glass full.

If you are particularly well behaved, the bartender might shake your hand. If you get the handshake, be skeptical. And, until you've collected more information, remain skeptical. There are two kinds of bartender handshakes. There's the handshake that is meant to promote or reward tipping. And there's the handshake that means "You have made my shift more pleasant, thank you." Since there is virtually no way to distinguish between them, the handshake is not a reliable barometer of anything, including whether or not you have found your place.

Looking the bartender in the eyes when you order helps with the relationship. Like, directly in the eyes. A lot of people don't do that.

Some people don't say "Thanks" either.

However, the problem with having a place—especially if that place was the bar at San Domenico circa 2005—is that drinking there becomes very comfortable. And when drinkers become comfortable, they tend to drink a lot.

There were many instances early on in my time at *Esquire* (and San Domenico) when I drank too much. New York is conducive to this. You're not driving home, after all. But also: I felt like I needed to relieve the pressures of the job and the weirdness of living in New York.

My first two years of work in New York were all consuming. I worked a lot. I would stay 'til seven or eight every night and then walk over to the bar; then I would take the subway home and sit on my windowsill, with my feet on my fire escape, and smoke cigarettes. I'm not a smoker. Even when I was a smoker I wasn't a smoker. I only did it because it's odd to sit on your windowsill just staring out. (The only true virtue of smoking is it gives a purpose to people with nothing to do.) So I smoked. Which allowed me to get to know my neighborhood. I saw fights. I saw a bike being stolen. I saw a drug deal go down and then five minutes later I saw both seller and buyer rushed and arrested by a van full of cops. I saw NYU students walking in hormonal packs from party to party. I saw people who were *so* much more drunk than me. I saw and heard motorcycle gangs tear down Eighth Street in the middle of the night. I saw late-night public sex in the doorway of a store across the street. I saw a man pushing a shopping cart nonchalantly walk out into the middle of the street, pull down his pants, and empty his bowels as if it were a perfectly acceptable method of excretion. I saw New York.

Anyway, I felt I deserved a drink. And so I drank. And occasionally while drinking I pulled out a pen and scribbled notes about ideas we had.

Using a bar to relieve stress is easy. Using it as a satellite office requires certain rules. For some suggestions, see the next chapter.

25

How to Work While Drinking

Now, to work and drink effectively, you must understand what kind of work alcohol is conducive to. And when you want to know what kind of work alcohol is conducive to, you must look to the scientists. Because, amazingly, they've studied it. And here's what they've found out:

A Swedish psychologist suggests that although drinking may hinder things like organizing and actually executing your project (be it a book, a presentation, whatever), it can play a role in generating insights and helping "incubate" ideas along the way. In these stages, he writes, alcohol may contribute "toward release of the 'thought-flow.'"

University of Illinois psychology researchers have recently shown that men who had been drinking vodka–cranberry juice cocktails until their blood-alcohol content was just below the legal limit solved word-association problems faster and were more often correct when compared to a sober group. The next year the researchers found that slightly inebriated people were better at noticing small changes in a series of images but worse on memory problems.

What the Americans found is what the Swedes found: Alcohol *can* make you better at certain kinds of work. It helps you focus on nuances and lets ideas flow more freely, which are activities you want during a brainstorming session. So make sure you're pairing the right kind of work with the right kind of drinking.

Here Is Work You Should Not Do While Drinking

- Surgery
- Cheese making
- Mixed martial arts
- Decal application
- Trapeze artistry

Here Is Work You Should Do While Drinking

- Brainstorming new surgical methods
- New cheese development
- Trash talk
- New decal design
- "Hey, Enzo, what if we add a fifth guy?!"

Drinking is conducive to working. But mainly for brainstorming.

*   *   *

Lots of people subscribe to the notion.

The Persians drank while running an empire. Herodotus tells us that they would "deliberate upon affairs of weight when they are drunk; and then on the morrow, when they are sober, the decision to which they came the night before is put before them by the master of the house in which it was made; and if it is then approved of, they act on it; if not, they set it aside."

Churchill drank while waging a war. When staying at the White House in 1941, for example, he requested he be provided with a tumbler of sherry before breakfast, a few Scotch and sodas before lunch, and French champagne and ninety-year-old brandy before bedtime. And yet, he declared, "I have taken more out of alcohol than alcohol has taken out of me."

For a slightly more straightforward take, let us look to occasional philosopher and full-time Major League Baseball catcher A.J. Pierzynski: "Sometimes [during the game] you're just really struggling and you just say, 'Hey, you know what? I need something to calm me down and let's have a beer.'"

Working while drinking only works if you are not, uh, drunk.

After years and years of working and drinking at the

same time, I have developed a system for not getting drunk. I am unveiling it here for the first time. Here are the steps.

1. Don't drink too much.
2. "Do you guys serve food?"

Drunkenness is not the goal. Alleviation is the goal—of burdens, the pressures of office politics, actual work. Drinking while working is about *ideas.* You don't need to create. You just need to clear your mind. And it doesn't take much alcohol to do that. So you'll be having two drinks this afternoon, at most.

I learned to drink at San Domenico. I learned, over time (not at first . . . at first I was very sloppy), how not to drink too much.

What I learned can be distilled into a few simple rules that guided me then and still guide me today. Helpfully they all involve the number 20.

The Drinker's Rules of 20

Drink 20 percent less than you want to.

Speak at 20 percent of the volume you think is appropriate.

Say 20 percent fewer thoughts than you think you should share.

If Matchbox 20 comes on, ask the bartender if he can switch it to a different song.

And leave 20 minutes before you think you should.

Drinking while working should involve restraint and enthusiasm at the same time. You could have had *more*, but you're just having this much. You could have had *less*, but you're having this much.

When you drink, you will find yourself loosening up, of course. You will find yourself being forthright. There is a point during any period of drinking at which you are inebriated enough to have acerbic thoughts but prudent enough to not utter them. This is the moment you want to maintain. You want to be able to roll out blunt points responsibly. Irresponsibility is as grave a sin now as it was when you were sitting at your desk an hour ago. So, you maintain. And you listen way, *way* more than you talk. Which is always a good idea in a meeting—with drinks or without.

I've found the best way to maintain is to have exactly one drink.

That always seemed to be the plan. We'd just never stick to it. Drinking would always begin with Curc walking by my desk and saying, "Let's get a drink." I knew a drink would become two or three or four drinks, and then you have to decide if you're gonna grab another one and you do and then things get dicey. That's when you start jabbing people in the shoulder with your forefinger when trying to make a point, indiscriminately text people to tell them you miss them, and/or sing.

But I love drinking one drink. Or at least one drink as Renato served it, which involved a very stiff pour. At San Domenico the drink was always about two drinks. But still, it was one glass with one measure of liquid in it. That counts as a drink.

One drink feels like you're getting away with something. You're not impaired. You're not going to say anything regrettable—at least not because of the alcohol. You're not going to talk too loud. You're not going to feel hungover tomorrow. You're not spending too much money. You're not wondering why that person over there won't stop looking over at you and, interestingly, seems to have a similar sense of style as you and is glaring now, what the—oh, that's a mirror. (Happened once!) One drink is the just the right amount.

26

How to Begin a Work Thing

The thing I didn't understand early on in my career is: **The work party is not a party. It's an offsite meeting with free alcohol.** The venue is one of your office's many embassies, just like the Greek place across the street, the coffee bar at 7-Eleven, the bleak courtyard where people go to talk on their cell phones to prospective employers about other jobs. You may not technically be in the office, but you're still working.

You're also drinking.

When drinking is involved the focus tends to be on what we do while we're drinking—the things we say, how loud we say them, how much we drink. But the focus should be on what bookends the drinking: the decisions we make at the beginning and end of the party. If you get the bookends right, the middle is easy.

The workplace is full of guidelines. The work party needs guidelines as well. Maybe even more so.

The first thing you want to establish at a work party is the thing we always want to establish when we are working: the freedom to leave pretty much whenever we want to.

Say hello to the people you need to say hello to as early as possible. Beeline to the boss, the host, and other people you know you want to speak with.

Position yourself near where the food is or near the room the food comes out of. Eat early and often. Chicken lollipop? Why, thank you. Miso-cod slider? Indeed. Short-rib-and-lobster-foam napoleon? I'll take two.

Now you're ready to drink. Because you've basically had dinner.

Drink immediately. Then nurse a second drink. Have a third or fourth drink if you must, but don't think of the open bar as a buffet of alcohol. It's a mess hall of alcohol. You go, you get your ration, you go back to the party. Otherwise, you're seven glasses of brandy punch in and all of a sudden you're wearing reindeer antlers around your chin, open-mouth winking everyone, doing the Electric Slide, and referring to other people as "some of that."

Ration.

And then: Enjoy yourself.

And then: Leave.

* * *

What, you want to stay? Oh, no, you should just go.

You don't want to go? Read the next chapter, and then decide.

27

How to End a Work Thing

You will never regret leaving a work party early. So leave.

Now.

Just leave.

Are you ready to go?

No?

Great, then you should leave. You should always leave a work event before you're ready to go. One of the effects of alcohol is thinking you're having a better time than you actually are. Another effect of alcohol is delayed regret. So go.

Here is how you do it: Do not tell anyone you're leaving. No one needs to know you're heading out. Because no one cares. Don't say good-bye. Don't make a big deal about it. Just go. Don't go over there and say bye to your boss. You talked to your boss when you got here. Does he look like he wants to hear from you right now? So go.

This is the Irish Exit. The Irish Exit involves simply

leaving without saying good-bye. It's unclear why this is referred to as the Irish Exit. Because in Ireland, people love saying good-bye. It's an art form. Thus, good-byes can take forever. The Irish Exit may be the result of Irish people trying to avoid the Irish Good-bye.

Anyway, we don't have time for that right now. Just walk outside and don't come back. No one is keeping track of you. No one is going to wonder where you are. Trust that you will be glad you did it this way. Not now, but tomorrow.

End this party as you began it: by leaving.

28

Should You Be Dancing at This Work Thing?

Please choose one answer for each question and add up the points to find out if you should be dancing at this work thing.

1. How long has the party been going on?

A. *Just started (25)*

B. *Couple hours (4)*

C. *No idea (2)*

2. Pick the word that best characterizes your feelings about dancing, generally.

A. *Stupid (8)*

B. *Other (4)*

3. What genre of music is being played?

A. *Reggae (6)*

B. *Not reggae (8)*

4. Have you ever been employed as a dancer?

A. Yes (0)

B. No (8)

KEY

Any number of points: You should not be so much as bobbing your head at this work thing.

29

How to Give a Toast

I'm always impressed by people giving toasts.

You can stammer. You can forget to include people. You can go on too long. But if you're trying to eke out a thoughtful few words about someone else? Cheers to you, friend.

My personal toasting rate rose dramatically after I started working in New York, which is a toast-y sort of place. In the past ten years, I've listened to many. I've given many. Anniversary dinners. Going-away drinks. Celebratory conference-room gatherings. It's important to stand up, get sentimental, and clink glasses every now and then. A great toast is one of the most memorable and moving public performances regular people get to deliver. And they're incredibly effective morale boosters—precisely because they fall outside the normal life of an office. Toasts are way stations of goodwill and respect. And the object of the toast will never forget it.

The toast should come early. Maybe it's not the first thing, but it should happen near the beginning.

It's OK to yell at people to get them to be quiet.

You have to be standing up.

You have to hold your drink chest high during the entire toast.

If, while holding your drink chest high during the entire toast, your arm gets tired, then it's probably time to wrap it up. Arm fatigue is a natural toast timer.

Note: Do not hold up your toasting arm with your other arm in order to lengthen the toast. Best just to wrap it up, Sinatra.

Stay in one place. Leave "working the room" to the motivational speakers.

Any sort of "traditional Irish toast" that you found on the Internet is not recommended. Hearing "May your neighbors respect you, trouble neglect you, angels . . . inspect you" (or whatever it is the angels do to you in that toast) is not all that inspiring or touching outside of a cozy pub in Cork.

A single word of guidance: pithy.

I've found that the only thing you have to worry about leaving out is the names of people. This can be avoided by not naming *anyone*. I was once asked by my boss to give a toast to an assembled group of regular *Esquire* writers, all of whom I admire. I mentioned one writer as an embodiment of whatever point I was making. Then I saw the writer next to him, who was just as much of an embodiment, so I mentioned that guy too. Why stop there? So I mentioned the writer next to him. Then I mentioned one of my fellow editors. By the time I was done, I'd named about twenty people. I might have mentioned the waiter. What started out as a toast became a pointless exercise in naming people. I pretty much called attendance. Careful with names.

You could say: "To all of you." Which is concise. You could say: "Without your work, where would we be?" Which is vaguely gracious. You could say: "Give yourselves a round of applause." Which buys time. You could say: "Steve. [pause] Steve, Steve, Steve, Steve, Steve." Which buys even more time and puts all the attention on Steve.

If you say all that, then what you've got there is a toast. A real toasty toast. An empty, meaningless, limp toast. (Steve might disagree.) Which is fine. But just remember: A toast is an opportunity. It's a message. It's a tiny speech. And if it's good, people will remember it forever. But only if you keep one thing in mind: What you're really going for when you're toasting to a group of people is sentiment. When it comes to toasting, humor is overrated. Sentiment is the thing.

I interviewed Don Rickles a few years back and he said

this about giving a toast (I'm paraphrasing): "Prepare nothing. Do kindness at the end." Which is easy for him to say because, for Rickles, what comes in between the preparation and the kindness is: shtick. But shtick is tricky. In order to pull off shtick you have to be either a professional comedian or a nonprofessional comedian who could make it as a professional comedian if you applied yourself. Shtick requires ridicule and mockery in order to work. Shtick dies if it doesn't offend a little bit. That's the whole point of shtick. And that's why it's hard.

The advisable thing, then, is to do kindness in the beginning, the middle, and the end. If humor comes—and it often magically does when we're being sincere—then it comes. Sometimes the absence of shtick can be as memorable as shtick itself. Sustained sincerity is a shocking thing. It's a memorable thing. When it comes to toasts, laughter is overrated.

Notes?

Sure, but no notes is better.

But what if I don't know what to say?

Of course you know what to say.

But what if I leave something out?

Nobody misses what they didn't know is supposed to be there.

But what if I want to drive home an important point and don't want to screw it up?

No one is really looking for a point. They're looking to be touched. (Related: No touching people during the toast.) The point of a toast is to get your audience to like themselves (and you) more than they did before you started speaking. A set of "toast notes," as the Toastmasters organization may or may not refer to them, is simply a catalog of things that may or may not mean anything to you. If you stand up with no notes, then whatever comes to you while you're speaking is de facto sincere.

Think about the toast beforehand. Maybe make some notes in your office. But when you're standing up there in front of everyone: no notes.

Imagine you're not standing up among your peers. Pretend you're talking to someone at a barbecue. What would you say to that person about these people? Figure out what that would be, mostly leave out anything negative, and there's your toast.

A toast should be nontransferable. It should be about what you're feeling right now as you're standing up and looking at people you admire, and maybe even, you know, *like*. That's why a great toast can be constructed with only a few words. Toasts don't need to be *big:* all encompassing and profound. You're not Henry V. Or Gene Hackman. The best way to ensure that a toast will produce fulsome feelings is to not attempt to be fulsome. What happens then is a surprise. They're surprised. You're surprised. The waiters are surprised. A toast should reveal as much to you as it does to the people you're toasting.

The best part is, no matter how much you think you've mangled things or left something out or misquoted some "wise man," a toast is predetermined to end in the best possible way: with a drink.

30

Things You Should Never Say While Giving a Toast

"Furthermore . . ."

"Uhhhhhhh . . ."

"Whenever the occasion arose, he rose to the occasion."

"Let us bow our heads."

"And it goes something like this . . ."

"In closing . . ."

"Lo, though we entered a raging river . . ."

"Sure is toasty in here."

"Drinketh . . ."

"I told you to shut up."

31

How to Give a Speech When You're Terrified of Giving a Speech

Toasting is one thing. Speaking in front of people without a drink in your hand is entirely different.

As you advance in your career, opportunities to speak in public increase. You have to present something to the entire staff. You have to participate in a "panel discussion." You have to go give marginally useful advice to some college students.

The thing that happens to me is: I have a hard time swallowing. Amazing how many times a minute we swallow. We don't think about it. We just do it. When I have to give a speech, I become conscious of swallowing, and then I get anxiety about making it happen, and then I just . . . can't . . . make it happen. This is a problem. I have to stop, grimace, and try to force it. Then I become out of breath because, as I was trying to swallow, I stopped breathing. Now I'm out of breath after having done this weird mini-convulsion, and this is just not working and I want to walk off the stage and out of the building and into my apartment and under the sheets.

It used to be an almost crippling anxiety. Once, before a panel discussion, I took a big swig of vodka straight from a bottle in my freezer at eight fifteen in the morning, figuring that the buzz would relax my nerves in the short term but would wear off by the time I had to speak at nine. (Yes, I realize this is a warning sign.) I moved on to Xanax, which had the same effect, only it lasted throughout the speech.

The problem with medicating anxiety for public speaking is that I found it numbed the qualities that I needed to be an effective speaker: focus and enthusiasm.

What helped me the most, though, was to understand that A. public speaking can be accomplished by using certain rules, and B. *really* effective public speaking involves ignoring those rules and simply talking. Ultimately, a speech is a conversation—with a whole lot of people who are refusing to participate in the chat.

You're never going to get to B without a ton of practice— without simply doing a lot of speeches. So for now, here are the rules that have helped me the most:

Use a formula to write the speech.

There are so many to choose from: You could do the ol'

chestnut: 1. Tell them what you will tell them. 2. Tell them. 3. Tell them what you just told them.

You could do Dale Carnegie's so-called Magic Formula: 1. Tell a vivid personal story related to the topic. 2. Recommend one specific action for the audience to take. 3. Explain clearly and concisely how they will benefit from taking that action.

You could do the Churchill: 1. Pour gin into a mixing glass and, instead of adding vermouth, turn toward France and salute, then stir with ice and strain into a martini glass. Drink. 2. Start off strong and surprising—with a quote or a story. Drink. 3. Stick to one message that can be expressed in a single sentence and make it the focus of your talk. Drink. 4. Use simple language. Drink. 5. Be descriptive. Drink. 6. End with a bang. Drink.

You could do the TED Talk: 1. Open with a personal story that explains why this topic is important to you. 2. Tell another personal story. 3. And another. 4. Reach peak self-satisfaction that you're killing this TED talk. 5. Draw a surprising conclusion from the stories that can be expressed in a single sentence that people will want to immediately share on social media.

The formulas are different, but the common thread is: simplicity, poignancy, repetition.

Speak under your allotted time. **No one has ever**

walked away from a speech and said, "I wish that had been about two minutes longer."

Throughout the speech, look at five people, one in each corner and one in the middle. No, really, look at them. Talk *to* them. Imagine that you are answering a question that all five of them asked. Address them. Occasionally say "you." "I'm happy to be here" is a much less engaging message than "I'm happy to be here talking with you."

Open your mouth wider than normal. Like the opera singers do.

Wider.

Speak louder.

Louder.

Know that everyone is on your side. They want this to be interesting as much as you do. They want you to succeed.

OK, that's way too loud.

32

Things You Should Never Say During a Speech

"A great man once said..."

"It all started back in..."

"Folks..."

"At the end of the day..."

"Sorry. I get a little emotional."

"So then I says to the lady, 'Hey, lady!...'"

"I know we're running out of time, but I just have twelve more points to make."

"This armored scythe stroke almost reached Dunkirk! *Almost*, but not quite. We shall fight on the beaches..."

"...And I'm here to tell you: That great man was me."

"Now, if you'll excuse me for a moment, I'll be over here attempting to swallow."

33

How to Give a Speech When You Have Just Taken One Too Many Xanax

O K. We're gonna do this together. I'm here for you. Now . . . I know how you feel. It's like you've just eaten a pot brownie, chased it with Wild Turkey 101, and then popped one-third of a Unisom. You're disoriented but totally aware of your responsibilities, and . . . zzzzz.

Wake up!

First, can you swallow at will? Yes? Great.

Can you say the ABCs? Yes? Great.

Can you stand on one leg? Yes? Great.

Can you believe that Hall and Oates has never gone by that name and has always referred to themselves as "Daryl Hall and John Oates"? No? It's true.

What you want to do is:

Take a walk around the block. Get your oxygen levels up, get your neurons firing.

Stand up straight, which opens the chest, which makes it easier to . . .

Breathe deeply. From your abdomen, not your throat.

Memorize your first sentence. Have it written down. But if you have to read it, read it. The intro is a gateway. Nail it, and you're halfway there.

And remember: They're all rooting for you. Everyone wants to enjoy themselves. Everyone wants to be amused and educated. Everyone wants you to do well. (Which brings up an important point: **In business, you must assume that everyone is rooting for you.** Are there sometimes people in the room who wish you would fail? Yes. Can you ever confirm that this is the case? No. Then assume the best and move on. Not just for this speech. In the meeting, in the hallway, at the microwave when you feel an icy stare from the weird guy making his tea—every day you go to work, assume that everyone is on your side. Don't saddle yourself with presumptive animosity.)

And understand that no one knows that you are compromised. No one.

Now, get out there.

Hang on. Stand on one leg again just to make sure. See? You're perfect.

34

How to Talk to "Important" People

"Important" is a tricky word. In my career, important has meant notable. Or famous, even. It's also
meant people who have been important for my career, which
includes the famous people but also includes many types of
colleagues—assistants, peers, bosses, possible future bosses—
as well as people in my professional orbit: PR people, other
media people. These are people who mean a lot to me, whose
relationships I value—even if they don't know my name and
even if it's a onetime encounter. When I profiled Rihanna for
Esquire in 2011, she was not only important to me because
she was a superstar—she was important because I saw her
as my first chance to write an in-depth story of an interesting
person for *Esquire*. I decided there would be a lot at stake
with that assignment. But my writer-subject relationship
with Rihanna is no less important to my career than my professional relationship with a talented, dedicated assistant
who helps me do better work. Both relationships could lead

to great things—for them and for me. What follows are tips for talking to people who are important to me. While some of these examples are highly specific—some are even, uh, particular human beings—hopefully each contains a lesson for talking to the important people in your own life.

Counterpart at Another Organization

Give up a little information. Don't stay buttoned up. Relax. It's weak to be aloof around the competition. That suggests you're nervous. A competitor isn't a permanent enemy but a potential colleague and ally.

Someone Who Has Asked You an Indiscreet Question About Your Company at a Party

Pick one:

"You never know."

"Hard to say."

"It depends on so many factors."

"You gotta do what you gotta do."

"What led to you wondering about that?"

"But don't you think that's only part of the story?"

"We do what we can."

Bartender

A shift has occurred over the past ten years or so. We used to talk to bartenders about our problems. Now we talk to them about our homemade bitters and the drink they just made for us and that bottle of obscure rye. So talk about your problems. Or ask them what theirs are.

Supermodel

The first cover story I wrote for *Esquire* was a profile of super-model Bar Refaeli for the July 2009 issue. She was *Esquire*'s cover model for an inspired mash-up of photography, super-model, fiction, and body paint. The photos that were going to be shot later that day would accompany a Stephen King short story, the first words of which would appear on the cover of the issue . . . because they would be painted on her nude body. Which is how I came to sit with her alone in the cold, on a bench outside Chelsea Piers, a large multiuse complex on the Lower West Side of Manhattan that houses sports facilities and photo studios, watching her smoke.

I wasn't used to interviewing famous people—Refaeli wasn't crazy famous, but her relationship with Leonardo DiCaprio was ongoing and she was the most famous person I'd ever interviewed. So I was nervous.

We sat on a bench together, looking out over the gray river. She wore little makeup. She had on a flannel shirt and leggings. She smoked. Her natural frown seemed even frownier in person. We were a journalist and supermodel in downtown Manhattan, but we looked like a couple in a fight waiting for a bus in Bend, Oregon.

Maybe she was bored by the questions. I sure was.

The problem with interviewing celebrities is that they are primed mostly to talk about their "projects." That's the implicit agreement. You give us time. We'll get your project in the story. And that just isn't very interesting. Talking about a "project" amounts to marketing speak. They've rehearsed their talking points. They don't want to go off script.

This isn't always true. The exception among actors is comedic actors, who are invariably great interviews, because they think about great answers for a living. An interview for them is just a series of prompts that allows them to try out new material. Chris Rock is probably the best at this. Patton Oswalt and Louis C.K. are great at it, too.

The pressure to ask people about things I'm not inherently interested in has a strange effect. I develop temporary personality disorder. As I hear myself speak, it doesn't sound like me. My mouth is moving and there are sounds coming out, but the voice is not mine. It's like the voice of a cousin—one who isn't very intelligent and says "totally" way too much. I disassociate.

And as a result the interview was boring, awkward, lifeless.

After fifteen minutes I'd run through all the questions on my notecard. Not knowing what else to say, I asked her: Uh, how do you model? Like, how do you do it?

"What do you mean?"

How does it work? What are the skills involved?

"There are tricks. The palm of the hand—you need to make it long, your fingers long."

She made a claw shape with her fingers and unfurled them. She extended her leg like a ballerina so her foot was part of one graceful line. She somehow made her collarbone more prominent.

As she talked about the work of modeling, she stood up and actually did her work. It was a technical thing to look at. She didn't seem more beautiful. She just seemed more lithe, tall, connected to what she was standing on, more a part of her environment, more confident. The way to make the most of a conversation with a famous person is the way to talk to anyone: You think of the thing that they do all day long but that no one ever asks them about. Their answers will be rich and substantive because they have thought about these things every way there is to think about them. The singer has tons of thoughts on rehearsal, on how to stalk a stage, on looking at fans. The plumber has tons of thoughts on gravity. The insurance agent has tons of thoughts on risk. And the model has tons of thoughts on the body—not only what you do with your arms and legs but what you do with your fingers and toes.

People love talking about what they *actually* do for a living. Not their *jobs* but their work.

Supermodel When She's Nude and the First Few Words of a Stephen King Story Have Been Applied to Her Body and You Need to Proofread Her Because You're the Only Qualified Person in the Photo Studio to Do So

Hey, man, can you, like, read her?

Pardon?

Like, can you read her, and make sure everything's right?

Eye contact, eye contact, eye contact. You walk over to Bar Refaeli and smile. Eye contact. You will not receive a smile back because she is nude on a hard platform with a Stephen King story applied to her body and someone she barely knows is sheepishly saying, "I'm just gonna read you if you don't mind?" Despite the lack of reciprocity, you should keep smiling. Abandon eye contact. Keep smiling. Read her three times. Remember to check for punctuation. Say thank you and good-bye.

Someone Crying at Work

Understand that crying is part of an important physical response to stress that makes us feel better. As intense and sad as it appears, crying is the beginning of feeling better. And so let them cry. Do not say, "Please stop crying." or even "There's no need to cry." Crying is cathartic. You don't want to suppress it. But do not acknowledge the crying. Speak as if there is no crying. And keep speaking until they stop crying or excuse themselves. And take the focus off them. Talk about once being in a similar situation. Tell a parable if you have to. Recite the Gettysburg Address if you have to, but keep talking. Take the spotlight, which only increases their embarrassment and likely mortification, off them.

Radio and TV Host

Don't think about the audience. Think about the interviewer. Focus on every word the interviewer says. This will be easy because you are, for the purposes of the interview, the most important person in the world. What makes for a good interview—on both sides—is focus, engagement, and polish. Talk as if you're on a great first date, as if you think everything being said is brilliant and funny and original. Seem as interested in the questions as you are in your answers. Listen.

Famous Rapper

Standing in the entryway of the G-Unit record label offices at Forty-First Street and Eighth Avenue, I was a little, uh, jumpy.

I was interviewing Curtis "50 Cent" Jackson for *Esquire*'s long-running "What I've Learned" feature, which includes only the words of the interviewee—wisdom from a life well lived. So you have to go deep with the interview. You have to prompt introspection. I was going to ask him about his music, but I was also going to ask him about his mother's death when he was a little boy, his life of crime (or "hustling," as it's always vaguely put), and being shot nine times in a matter of seconds, and lots of things that might be considered, uh, delicate. This is a man who raps the line "Many men wish death upon me, blood in my eye, dawg, and I can't see" without irony. So I was nervous. Not to mention the G-Unit offices were in the middle of a renovation, and his entire staff was wedged into one or two rooms, and the only available space for the interview was a room under construction. Workers walked in and out, and there was sawing, drilling, hammering, angle grinding.

And then I met him.

Meeting 50 Cent (it's "Fifty" not "Fiddy," he confirmed to me) is an encounter defined by one thing. His smile.

How to describe the toothy smile of 50 Cent in person? Let's see: Imagine forty kittens winking. Or a sunflower giving you a thumbs-up. Or a panda saying "Nice to meet ya!" as he tips his hat because this panda is dressed like Dick Van Dyke in the "strolling in the park" scene in *Mary Poppins.*

As we shook hands (full palm, moderate pressure), still smiling, he said, "This is going to be an interesting interview."

Note: If you are ever interviewed by a journalist or anyone else, this is a useful way to start things off. Because it accomplished three important things.

1. It disarmed me. (Celebrity interview subjects never, ever, ever say stuff like that before interviews. Usually what they say is: "Nice to meet you" in a way that suggests that it isn't. And then stare at you in a way that you stare at the wall when you're getting examined by a doctor.)

2. It guaranteed a positive outcome.

3. It said to me: "I have thought about this. And it matters."

He may say that to all the writers, but it's a hell of a line. And it made me relax.

And I needed to relax.

As we were talking, every time the drilling, hammering, grinding, would start up, he would simply grab the recording device and hold it up to his mouth as he spoke. It was a subtle, thoughtful, helpful thing. And it suggested that he was a partner as much as a subject.

I love reading the piece that resulted from the interview. Not just because of this: "Don't wait for them to tell you. Tell them." Or: "Hip-hop is arrogant because *people* are arrogant." Or: "Always have bail money." (Great tip!) But because the success of it depended on what 50 Cent suggested to me when we met: "You're important too." He wanted his time with me to matter. He wanted to be surprised and delighted. He wanted everyone to relax. He wanted a cohort. He wanted this to be interesting. And it was. The way to talk to important people is to recognize that you are their equal.

People Who Are Bored in a Meeting

When people speak in a meeting you're leading, lock in on what they say. Listen. This suggests to everyone in the room not only that they're being heard but that they're accountable. The substance of what they're saying is being pondered, if not by everyone, by you. Which means things are at stake, which is intense, which wakes people up.

Moderately Famous Celebrity at a Party

I have no idea. I have tried and I don't know how to do this. Small talk doesn't seem to work. Neither does medium talk. Moderately famous celebrities are difficult. It's as if they're too new at being a celebrity to be confident and secure and too famous to be humble and interested in you.

Top Executives at Very Large Companies

Just listen. They have dominant personalities, and all they really want is for you to listen. They won't listen to you, so you might as well listen to them.

Famous Pop Star

Before I interviewed Rihanna, I read a book on the history of Barbados, the country she lived in until she came to the United States for the first time at sixteen years old. (The sugarcane industry there was pioneered by Jewish refugees. Who knew?) I listened to her music exclusively for three weeks. ("Pon de Replay" from her first album: underrated single.) I listened to any records she says influenced her. (The title track from Brandy's album *Afrodisiac* is a highlight.) I approached this interview as if I was her official biographer.

When I'm freaked out about a new task, I tend to overdo it. I go all in.

I do this kind of thing defensively. When I feel like I don't have a handle on what I'm doing, I try to "lock it down" by doing more research on and thinking more about the subject than can be justified, so that even if I will be proven incompetent, I will at least have been irrationally dedicated before failing. I did it with the in-flight magazine. I did it with my *Esquire* interview. And I did it with Rihanna.

The assignment was to profile the singer for the magazine's annual "Sexiest Woman Alive" feature, but as far as I was concerned it was going to be the first celebrity profile (not to mention the first magazine story) ever to win a Nobel Prize.

Normally for a story like this one, you get about ninety minutes with the subject in some coffee shop at around eleven in the morning on a Wednesday and then you write a short profile that alternates between telling the reader how the lunch is going ("She orders a croissant—languidly") and a little about her life ("It all started in Boise").

For this story I was getting only ninety minutes at a restaurant in LA, so I decided to "shadow" her. Shadowing sounds intriguing but it isn't. You just hang out wherever the subject is. You loiter, basically. To shadow Rihanna, I went to two of her stadium shows in the New York area— one on Long Island and one in New Jersey—hanging around backstage, talking to her publicist, the music producers who discovered her when she was fifteen, her manager, Kanye West, her wardrobe person, and her dancers, who were so full of manic energy that it was impossible to talk to them. Backup dancers have the general bearing of squirrels. And I flew to LA to do a short interview. And I begged my boss to allow me to go to Barbados a week after the interview to see her perform in her home country for the first time.

It was a little overboard. But I wasn't going to let lack of access be the reason the story sucked.

The interview took place a week after the Long Island show at her favorite restaurant in LA, an Italian place where the windows are blocked by shrubs. It caters to celebrities, and she eats there three or four times a week. When I arrived, five other women were with her. I approached the table and asked Rihanna if now would be a good time.

"Sure," she said.

And her entire party immediately and as a single unit decamped to another table.

Which was impressive.

After the usual pleasantries were exchanged, I explained to her how I was not going to be writing the typical celebrity profile. And certainly not the typical *sexy-lady* profile! No, this—*this!*—was going to be journalism, Ms. Rihanna Fenty of Bridgetown, Barbados. Journalism! Now, if you will, I have some questions to ask.

(It was slightly less "cub reporter in a thirties film" than that, but you get the idea.)

She looked at me with no discernible reaction to my bold prediction and asked, "Would you like some moscato?"

I larded the early part of the conversation with some Barbadian esoterica. But she didn't seem impressed. I asked her about the music industry, but she seemed bored. None of my questions seemed to work. It was not a good interview.

And then I asked her about her house growing up.

We didn't talk about "Barbados." We talked about the tiny house she grew up in, within earshot of the cricket stadium she would be performing at in a couple of weeks.

The only things that interested her were the specifics. The only things that interested *me* were the specifics. The details of life. What she *actually* does with her day.

It was delightful.

And her entire facial expression changed. Her body language went from "Another interviewer asking the same questions" to "I get to talk about something new."

She seemed relieved when I asked about being raised by her mother, about auditioning for two American music producers when she was fifteen, about staying with one of the producers and his family in Connecticut as she took meetings in New York trying to get a deal, about signing her first contract with Def Jam Recordings—literally signing the contract while seated at the head of a conference room table, wearing an all-white outfit, her smiling growing wider with each signature.

Remember: Important people have a past that involved them being not so important.

People Having Their First Day at Work

"Welcome and congratulations. We're all glad you're here." The congratulations part is big. Because it acknowledges that they've won something, which they have.

Politicians

One of the strangest story ideas I've come up with involved taking a photo crew to the Hyatt Regency Century Plaza in LA during the annual meeting of the US Conference of Mayors (it's a mayors' convention, basically) and photographing and interviewing as many mayors as we could. Small-town mayors. Big-city mayors. Men. Women. Humble public servants. Raging egomaniacs.

The idea was to present a snapshot of America through photographs and interviews of these men and women.

The whole thing was intimidating to me. I was going to be dealing with a lot of power in one room. Important people. Bosses.

As mayor after mayor streamed into the large meeting room where we'd set up, I learned very quickly how to talk to mayors. You ask them about their towns. The roads. The schools. You ask them about their responsibilities.

Some of those mayors have gone on to become US congressmen, important governors, possible presidential candidates. When I see them on TV, I think, "Hey, you were like a deer in the headlights during the photo shoot." Or, "Hey, you forgot to zip up your fly before coming out of the dressing room." Or, "Hey, you were sweating like crazy."

If you watch "important" people, you will see how they are just like you. You will see them stumble over their words, sneeze in a strange way, get spinach stuck in their teeth. You will occasionally be bored by what they're saying. You will watch them drop food in their laps. You will listen to them lose their train of thought. **Conversations— with "important" people and anyone else—are about seeing the human being, stripped of status.**

Interns

Say hello to them. Smile at them. Ask them what they're working on. Tell them how important they are. Because they are. And because they will not always be interns. They are future important people. They're already important. Be amiable to interns.

35

How to Think About Clothes

I am not a great dresser. Despite the fact that I work at a magazine that is a leading authority on men's fashion, I never will be "fashionable." It takes a lot of work to be fashionable. And I am too ambivalent to get myself to that point. I want to look "good." I don't care about looking "great." For the purposes of the next few chapters I will assume that this describes you too.

If you don't think you "care" about fashion, fine. But clothes matter. They have the power to change your outlook. They are representative of you, and ignoring that obvious truth is denying yourself a really powerful tool. (A lot of people who say they don't care about clothes spend a lot of time crafting an image that suggests that. Crafting that image involves the purchasing and wearing of clothes.)

*   *   *

About a year after I started at *Esquire*, my boss said to me, "I want you to start working with Nick." He wanted me to be the editorial liaison to the fashion department led by Nick Sullivan, the magazine's British-born fashion director. It's an important role because Nick Sullivan and his staff, despite being fine writers, are mainly tasked with setting the course for *Esquire* fashion coverage, not handling and moving copy. My job was to do the copy part. It wasn't crucial that I had a sense of fashion, but it would have been helpful. I was in no position to object to the clearly bad idea of pairing one of the magazine's worst dressers with its best, so I looked down at my square-toed shoes and said, "Uh, sure."

My first few weeks as the edit-fashion liaison consisted of trying to learn the technical things: How much cuff you should show at the end of your jacket sleeve (quarter inch) . . . What a suit's silhouette should look like (narrow, close) . . . Why you should never button the top button of a three-button suit (makes you look like a chauffeur) . . . If a sport coat or suit jacket isn't one large meal away from being uncomfortably tight, then it doesn't fit as well as it should . . . "Trousers." Yes. "Pants." Fine. "Slacks." No. . . . And the single most important rule of fashion: **Always cut a string, never pull.**

I thought I was just learning about clothes. But I was not just learning about clothes. I was learning about style.

And style is a lot more interesting. Because style is less about clothes than it is about ideas.

And its biggest idea, of course, is: confidence.

Confidence is hard to get a handle on. Some of us seem to be born with it. But research indicates it can also be shaped by how we think, how we carry ourselves physically, and even how we dress.

That last type of confidence—being related to concrete, physical, purchasable, wearable things—is highly attainable, of course. Which makes it an amazingly effective tool at work.

There is a phenomenon that's recently (and amusingly) been referred to by researchers at Columbia University as "enclothed cognition"—the effect of clothing on mental processes. Among other things, the Columbia researchers found that people who wore a doctor's coat showed higher attention to detail during a task than those in street clothes. The conclusion: Clothes can actually put you in a different psychological state. Think of your favorite shirt or dress. Its power doesn't lie so much in how it looks but how it makes you feel. And how it makes you feel is confident. After one of my first meetings with the fashion department, having made one too many self-deprecating comments about how I dressed, I was approached by one of the fashion editors, who asked me, "Would you like me to help you buy some shoes?" I said, "Thank you," with immense gratitude. Shopping is not something I enjoy. I feel like I need a guide for it just like I would if I were rafting down a river. So that evening, we walked to a few different stores on Fifth Avenue and I bought a nice pair of shoes. They were more than I'd ever spent on shoes. But they immediately made me feel more confident, more capable, more comfortable. They are cap-toe Oxfords with a slightly pointy toe. I don't know why I like them. But I know I feel more capable when I have them on.

I still wear them. I've had them resoled a few times and I get a shine every few weeks, but I still wear them and I've gotten more than my money's worth. These shoes became like the doctor's coat in that experiment. They transformed me in the same way praise from a coworker does, in the same way a raise does. But this is something *you* are doing for yourself. Wearing clothes that make you feel good—and capable and confident—is like giving yourself a promotion. You should do that every day. That kind of professional opportunity shouldn't be wasted.

36

Style Rules for Work That You Hear All the Time, Plus One You Never Do

The usual "how to dress" rules for the workplace go something like this:

- Gray and dark blue suits for men. Gray, dark blue, and black suits for women.
- No cologne or perfume.
- No wrinkles.
- Better to overdress than underdress.
- Go with solids, understated stripes, or small patterns.

These are acceptable rules but too prescriptive (and a little out-of-date).

The problem is: I don't know the fashion customs of your industry. Maybe you'd look out of place if you didn't wear a sport coat. Maybe you'd look out of place if you didn't wear a hoodie. Maybe you'd look out of place if you didn't wear a giant beaver outfit because your job is to anthropomorphize a sports team.

I don't know if you should wear that dress to the interview. But I do know that if, when you put that dress on, you feel like *they* need *you* more than you need them, then you're wearing the right dress.

(Nice dress.)

I eventually learned that employing the rules to find something you look good in and that gives you confidence is only the first step in the process. The next step is the adoption of a concept that blew my mind and forever changed how I look at style (and lots of other things in life).

37

Sprezzatura!

The concept of sprezzatura was introduced by sixteenth-century Italian courtier Baldassare Castiglione in *The Book of the Courtier,* a sort of Miss Manners guide for court during the Renaissance. From the text: "Avoid affectation in every way possible . . . [and] practice in all things a certain sprezzatura [nonchalance] so as to conceal all art and make whatever is done or said appear to be without effort and almost without any thought about it."

I first encountered it while writing the copy for a fashion story in *Esquire*'s biannual style guide *The Big Black Book.* As I reviewed the photos, I noticed that Sullivan had his subjects—real men, as was the magazine's way at the time, not models—wearing well-tailored suits, but in each photo something was a little bit "off." In one photo a collar was a little askew. In another, the subject wasn't wearing a belt. In another, the tie was "too short." In another, the shirt and tie seemed to "clash." The clothes were imperfect, messy. But the men looked fantastic.

This was a revelation. I felt the same way looking at this spread that I felt walking through the Modern Art Museum of Fort Worth years earlier and seeing Robert Rauschenberg's early nineties sculptures, which were beautifully ordered junk—old bicycle wheels and rusty toolboxes and discarded pieces of cardboard that looked as perfect to me as a Monet lily pond. The Rauschenberg exhibit was the first time I understood the power of art. The sprezzatura story in *The Big Black Book* was the first time I understood the power of style.

Sprezzatura allows for—and, more important, promotes— whimsy, messiness, flaws. Your tie is askew. Sprezzatura. Your shirt is a little untucked? Sprezzatura. Those prints don't mix? Sprezzatura. You're accidentally wearing your shirt inside out? Just call it sprezzatura and go about your day. Sprezzatura endorses comfort, individuality, contradiction, wrinkles. What the Italians are saying is (and this is a loose translation): "Give a shit. And then slightly less of a shit." Sprezzatura allows you to look formal and casual *at the same time.*

It's not just a way to think of style. It's a way to think of work. Your work and the social interactions that go along with it should not be perfect. I mean, they can't be. But also: They *shouldn't* be. Your work should be wrinkled. It should show wear and it should indicate that you're trying new things and taking chances. It should be slightly disheveled.

What I learned in the two years I worked with the fashion department is: **Style is ordered by rules, but it's not governed by them.** And your own approach to style is not complete without the confidence that will make it all come together. It's a symbiotic relationship: The clothes will help your confidence and your confidence will make the clothes look better. And over time—as short as just a few months—it builds and builds until people think of you as someone who looks like you know what you're doing—with clothes and with work. Sprezzatura is about acknowledging that perfection—in clothes and anything else—is impossible, and that to pursue it is folly. It's the mark of confidence, it's a guiding philosophy, and it's one hell of a mantra.

38

An Impostor's Garden of Mantras

I use "Sprezzatura" as a kind of mantra. I actually say
it out loud.

Someone else: "The ending of this story you're editing
is a little abrupt, don't you think?"

Me: "Sprezzatura."

You get the idea. It's both a dismissive response and an
advancing of philosophy.

Here are some other mantras that can help bridge the gap
between your talents and your self-confidence. Use as you like.

Who's a genius? [look in mirror] That guy.

This would be more stupid were it not for my involve-
ment.

I am quite talented.

I am slightly more than quite talented.

I am remarkably quite talented.

I bow to my self-confidence. (The original mantras involved a lot of "bowing.")

I bow to my talents.

I bow to my dignity.

You know what, I'm just gonna bow.

Hey, look. My favorite shoes.

I like my shoes.

They instill confidence in me.

I bow to my shoes.

To my shoes, I say: Thanks.

My shoes need a shine.

Sprezzatura.

Is a mantra like "Sprezzatura" sometimes a crutch?
Sure. But so is a Twix break. Does it give you license to ignore problems you don't feel like fixing? Yes. In this context,
is it as banal as "It is what it is"? Indeed. More important,
it's a useful thing to say to yourself when you're feeling a
little unsure about a problem. It liberates you from the
shackles of perfection. Also: It's fun to say. "Sprezzatura"
for everyone.

39

A Few Words About Collaboration

Most of the good ideas I've had in my career are the results of collaboration. And the collaborations that have proven to be the most fruitful have been ones that haven't involved a lot of niceties.

Every collaboration starts with either an implicit or explicit admission of weakness. You're admitting that you need each other, that you're better off together than you would be apart. Every collaboration begins as a *co-failure*.

If you're able to choose your cohort, then seek out a complement. A Jobs to your Wozniak, a "dominant" to your "conscientious," a rhino to your tickbird. You want someone who knows as much as you do, just not about the same stuff.

It helps if your collaborator is someone you're always on the verge of arguing with. Tension can produce wonderful things. It *has* to. Otherwise you're spending time with someone you find vaguely irritating and also doing bad work. Why not just do one of those things? The discomfort must be redeemed by greatness. Some of my best work has been done with people who are a little, uh, cranky. Some of my *fastest* work has been done with these people: I've found that when you work with someone who doesn't mind stepping on your toes or hurting your feelings, the communication is highly efficient, and you get to the good work faster.

So find a jerk, and go do something great together.

40

A Few Words About Credit

Early on, I made the mistake of telling one of my bosses what I did every day as a prelude to asking for a raise. He looked at me and said, "I know what you do."

The point he was making with both his words and his facial expression was: "You're better than this."

And I was.

I work at a magazine. And magazines involve a lot of delegation from the senior editors to the less senior editors. If you want full credit for everything you work on, then journalism is not for you. No office job is, really.

That's just not how things work when you're starting out—and to some extent, for your entire career. You support people. You support the institution. And the institution's ideas and mission. And you're not going to get a lot of explicit credit for that support.

Unless someone is scheming to receive credit for your work, it's best to let credit work itself out. Even if you're not being properly credited, you will seem small for asking for it.

(And if you're concerned that at the end of a collaboration you won't get specific credit for your specific ideas, realize that you won't get specific blame when your specific ideas don't specifically work out so well.)

41

How to Email

Workplace communication should involve as much civility as candor. **Kindness and consideration are important things for kind and considerate people to express. Except when it comes to email.**

The problem with pleasantries over email is that they take a long time to write and a long time to read. Writing— in an email or a magazine story—should be aggressive and clear above all other qualities.

So in order to increase the efficiency of a category of writing plagued by inefficiency—too many exclamation points, the obligatory "How are you?," indiscriminately cheery email signatures like "All my best"—I propose an emailing approach that amounts to a single question: "What would Robert De Niro type?" You get an email. You read that email. You respond to the email as if you were Robert De Niro. You will find that your email responses will involve messages like: "Sure" and "Great" and "Yes" and "No" and "Perfect" and "Sorry." Warning: Do not confuse the man with the characters he has played. Otherwise you'll be typing things like "Sit there. Don't move. Let it bleed."

You will also find that you might actually get on the phone with someone if the response requires too much typing. Bobby De Niro is not going to sit there and type a long email. He's going to pick up a phone and figure it all out. Or if the person you're emailing is in the office, you might find that you actually get up from your desk and go talk to that person face-to-face. Which is the best kind of communication.

And here's the best part: People may start emailing you *as if you are* the iconic American actor. Which means you won't have to suffer through so many pointless introductory thoughts like: "I hope you had an awesome weekend." You might not have to be confronted with so many exclamation points at the end of every sentence. You might not receive a five-hundred-word email that ends with the worst question of all time: "Thoughts?" Because you are Robert De Niro and people will learn to email you accordingly— with a sense of efficiency and purpose. (And possibly fear. But mostly efficiency and purpose.)

42

A Few More Rules for Emailing

Ask yourself if you would cc yourself. Easy with the cc.

Not only should you assume that every email you send will get forwarded to someone else; you should assume that every email you send will someday be read aloud in a court of law. Discretion.

If your message is fewer than seven words, put it in the subject line.

An email signature should not involve words of wisdom. Not Aristotle. Not Gandhi. Not Hayley Williams of the chart-topping rock band Paramore.

ALL CAPS. No.

SMALL CAPS. No.

wHaTeVeR YoU cAlL tHiS. Absolutely not.

When in need of a font that's the right mix of authoritative but discreet: Look to Helvetica.

Cambria? Please.

Say "thank you." There are many ways to say "thank you" over email. "Thanks," you could say. Or "TY." Or "Thx," if you must. There is also: "Thank you." In almost any other context, "thank you" isn't noteworthy. But you don't see it so much in emails, typed out like that. Which makes it a powerful message. It's simple, direct, meaningful, gracious. It almost seems extravagant. Which makes it memorable. And impossible to misinterpret.

43

Why Strident Postures on Social Media Are, at the End of the Day, Probably a Bad Idea—Especially if You're Looking for a Job

I tweet. A little. I'm not very good at it because my natural inclination is toward discretion and, if I'm being honest with myself, hedging in such a way as to make my position on something murky enough that no one can get too upset about it.

This doesn't work on, say, Twitter. Twitter rewards people who offer entertaining and concise takes. But "entertaining and concise" leaves room for "mocking and glib," which seems to work well on social media. But "mocking and glib" does not work so well in real life. And it really doesn't work in the workplace.

And it *really* doesn't work when a prospective employer is checking out your Twitter feed. Which will happen.

A 2014 CareerBuilder survey found that 51 percent of employers who research job candidates on social media said they've found content that caused them to not hire the candidate. It was 43 percent in 2013 and 34 percent in 2012. The top five reasons for rejecting a candidate based on social media were: provocative or inappropriate photographs or information; information about them drinking or using drugs; bad-mouthing their previous company or fellow employee; poor communication skills; discriminatory comments related to race, gender, religion, etcetera.

Another way to put it is that candidates are rejected for simply expressing who they are. For being frank, honest, open. For merely talking about when you woke up this morning, what team you root for, that you could totally use a foot massage right now, daylight savings whats up with that #toodamndark, and this lady behind you at the drugstore all like where is the candy corn lmao.

This information is valuable because it contains clues to how you *actually are*. But **employers don't want to know how you actually are. They want you to be the you that they want you to be.** They want you to fulfill the fantasy that they have in their head. They don't want you. They never wanted you.

Yet there you are on Twitter. Or at least some version of you.

Look, I know that we should all be ourselves. I've said as much earlier in this book. But even though you may think you are presenting yourself on Twitter, you aren't.

You are presenting yourself divided by the agenda of whoever is looking—especially when who is looking is your prospective employer.

Looking for a new employee is a necessarily hopeful process. Employers want you to be the "right one." When presented with vague information on a résumé, prospective employers tend to fill things in with positive information—information that originates from the fantasy they have of you. Your public social media accounts give them too much information to work with—information they might not be able to reconcile with the idealized version of you they have in their heads. Now, of course it says more about the skittishness of employers than it does about you. But the thing is: Your social media presence isn't you either. It's also a fantasy. And it might be a fantasy that an employer can't reconcile with the person they thought they wanted to hire.

If I may be frank: It would suck if your Twitter account—or your Facebook or Tumblr or whatever.blogspot.com is the reason someone soured on you. Maybe ultimately it would be a good thing—maybe you don't want to work for someone who lurks on social media looking for reasons to hate people. The key is to be aware of what's at stake.

44

How to Intimidate People

I have been told by former assistants that I can be "intimidating." The lack of smiling contributes to this image. So does having a fairly unemotional response to crises. And a default facial expression that reads as "unenthused." I don't entirely get it, but I have been told I'm intimidating.

Which I don't mind hearing.

I don't think intimidation is a bad thing. I don't think that feeling a little nervous in front of your boss or a coworker you respect *inherently* has a downside. It indicates that you feel like the relationship is important. As long as the one who is intimidating isn't actively trying to intimidate, then the intimidation seems like a natural and even beneficial by-product of a business relationship that matters —and out of which might come something great.

But what is it that makes people intimidating? What is

it that makes an intern a little on edge? What is it that makes you stumble over your words in front of your boss?

It could be that you're engaging in harassment. That's one way to intimidate. You could maliciously be causing an underling or a peer (or even a superior) to feel scared of some implicit or explicit threat you're making. But that's not what we're talking about. (And if that's something you think your behavior might be interpreted as, then you need to immediately stop that behavior and try to figure out what's driving it.)

You could be acting in an overconfident way. Overconfident people are perceived as having higher social status.

You could be rude. Rude people are perceived as having more power.

You could be tall. Tall people are seen as more intelligent, dominant, and healthy.

You could be attractive. Attractive people are perceived as smarter.

You could be a man with a shaved head. Men with shaved heads are seen as more dominant.

You could be a man with a beard. Bearded men are seen as having higher social status and being more aggressive.

You could have a deep voice. People with deeper voices are perceived as stronger and more competent.

You could be a great-looking, overconfident, rude, tall, bearded guy with a shaved head and deep voice. If you are, you're either legendary Scottish actor Sean Connery or Chicago-born rapper Common. And congratulations, you are really intimidating.

But in order to be intimidating in a way that isn't superficial, in a way that is connected to the quality of your work and comportment, you have to have the following things:

1. Your shit together, generally.

2. A belief in what you say.

3. Balls, whether man or woman. Metaphorical ones. At least the size of grapefruits. But not any larger than, say, the state of Oregon. (Balls the size of Jupiter or some other celestial sphere, while impressive, are really just a waste of balls.) Anyway, very large balls is what I'm saying. These balls must force you to take chances publicly. And you must have a record of your balls generally not steering you wrong. If you are intimidating people but you don't have balls, then you're an asshole.

4. And finally: empathy. You may intimidate but you may not intimidate without acknowledging what you're doing. And what you're doing is serious stuff. Research suggests that a social threat— here, feeling lesser in status—can set off the

same kind of fight-or-flight response as a physical threat. A flood of hormones such as adrenaline and cortisol makes us jittery and hampers
our ability to think logically and reflectively. You're
freaking people out when you intimidate them.
And you need to understand this. You need to act
upon that empathy. You need to do something
that will put the other person at ease. That will
lower their adrenaline levels, even if all you do is
say, "You're doing great," which will be a great
relief to the one you are intimidating. There's a lot
of power in the intimidation. And there is a lot of
power in mitigating it. If you have one without the
other, you're not doing it right.

But if you are able to do it the right way—if you can check
off those four boxes—then intimidation can be a very useful thing. It can establish order (just like it did back in junior high). It can establish status, which is a key part of
business—even if you wish it weren't. And it can establish
a clear path for decision making. Which is what *everyone*
wants in the workplace.

45

On Assholery

I am often mistaken for an asshole.

But I am not an asshole.

I'm a prick. Not all the time. But some of the time. I'm not proud of it. I try to be less of a prick in general. But that's just what I am sometimes at work: a prick.

Which is much more nuanced. Prickery is often the result of nerves and pressure, and its intensity fluctuates depending on the situation. It is often comical.

Assholes are not nuanced. They are assholes through and through. They are assholes when the pressure is on. They are assholes when the pressure is off. It's this lack of nuance that, helpfully, makes them easy to identify.

Here, a list of traits I've compiled both from years of working closely with assholes and from hours of reading the rich and burgeoning literature on assholery:

Narcissism. (I'm the most special of all of you.)

Overconfidence. (I can do anything.)

Impatience. (If I want it, I want it now.)

Aggressiveness. (Get out of my way.)

Recklessness. (Full speed ahead.)

Entitlement. (That's mine. Because it is.)

Delusion. (Who are you calling an asshole?)

Obliviousness. (Are you crying?)

Also: Utter predictability.

Which is why you should steer clear. If you sense that a prospective boss is an asshole, think about whether you want a narcissistic delusional aggressor having so much power over you. If a colleague is an asshole, know that they will never change.

But we cannot always steer clear. Assholes often disguise themselves as pricks or, even more slyly, as mensches and martyrs, before unleashing their assholery upon unsuspecting coworkers.

So, first, they must be accepted.

What you have to do is accept the assholery. Only then can you work with it. And you must work with it. They will not change.

This corruption places limits on the fruitfulness of your

collaborations. But in business, all we want is limits. When there is a project, do we not ask what the deadline is? What the budget is? How many people are involved? We should also want to know how many assholes are involved. Accept them.

Second, they must be embraced.

I find assholery to be banal, almost quaint. While it is awful, it is also very simple. And it's the assholes' intractability that makes me like having them around.

Here is why assholes are helpful:

1. They allow us to feel morally superior.

2. They are rallying points and morale boosters.

3. They contribute to the overall efficiency of the office. Because they are predictable, we can always account for their behavior ahead of time. You always know where you stand with an asshole. Beneath them, but still.

This works only if you are able to control your rage and understand that you are responsible for your reaction.

Third, they must be engaged.

No one is more surprised by confrontation than an asshole. But they must be confronted.

This is a moral matter, sure, but I assure you it has

practical implications. And the implications are only benefi-cial to you.

It cannot get worse. Assholes make every situation as bad as it can possibly be. That's why they're assholes. They pull the social rug out from everyone they're dealing with. They are 100 percent awful at all times.

So you have nothing to lose. Engage them. But not willy-nilly. Assholes are adept at squashing most pleas.

Here is the question that has worked for me.

"Why would you do that?"

This forces the asshole to account for their assholery. And because assholery cannot be accounted for, it is an impossible question to answer. This flummoxes the asshole. And a flummoxed asshole is a sight to behold.

Why would you do that? And they stammer something out. So you ask: "Right. But *why* would you do that?" And they look at you like you just asked them to solve a theorem. And so you ask, "To put it another way, why would *you* do *that?*"

You are forcing upon them a question that they never ask themselves.

You haven't taught them anything. That is not the point. The point is to tell them: I see what you are up to. You are making them slightly self-aware. And self-awareness to the asshole is water to the Wicked Witch, a proton torpedo to the Death Star's thermal exhaust port, a gust of wind to Donald Trump's hair.

We think of them as strong and destructive. While they are destructive, they are not strong. Their obliviousness makes assholes so odious, but it's this obliviousness that makes them so weak and easily flustered.

No, assholes are easy. It's the pricks you need to watch out for.

46

Are You an Asshole?

Select the answers that apply and add up the points to determine if you are an asshole.

Hi there!

Hi! (–5 points)

Hi. (0)

Yeah? (5)

Upon whose terms must all social interaction happen?

Mine (10)

The community of citizens (–5)

How many of these traits have you exhibited in the last hour? Circle all that apply.

Narcissism (2)

Impatience (2)

Aggression (2)

Entitlement (2)

Delusion (2)

Obliviousness (2)

Predictability (2)

Where are you on your journey?

Maneuvering my way to the top (1)

Picking off enemies (3)

Raging at imagined obstacles (5)

At the top, finally! (7)

Derailed (9)

Falling hard (15)

Just pluggin' away here! How's your journey, friend?! (–20)

Which of the following things do you typically not give?

A shit (1)

A damn (3)

A fuck (5)

A rat's ass (7)

A darn (–3)

Fill in the blank: "I am _____ than you."

"Better" (4)

"So much better" (6)

"Obviously totally better" (8)

"Maybe a little taller? Hard to say." (−4)

Your boss denies you a raise. You:

Figure that you just haven't done great enough work (−6)

Are taken aback by the rejection (2)

Just stare into your boss's eyes because obviously this is some sort of joke (5)

A right must be:

Argued for (−2)

Assumed (2)

Have you ever once—just once—posted a seething Yelp review?

Yes (30)

No (0)

If life were a band, which member of the band would you like to be?

Bassist (1)

Drummer (3)

Guitarist (5)

Lead singer (10)

Lead singer and occasional tambourinist and why aren't there any Starburst in my dressing room, man, like, how many times do we have to go over this, hey, girl, what's your name? (20)

May I borrow your pen?

Sure. (0)

I guess. (2)

Pick a Steve:

Carell (–5)

Buscemi (0)

Jobs (5)

Which of the following have you ever done? Circle all that apply.

Specified a premium vodka while ordering a dirty martini. (2)
Specified a premium vodka while ordering a very dirty martini. (4)
Cut in line to specify a premium vodka while ordering a very dirty martini. (6)

Complete this colloquialism: Before we move forward on this, it's important to walk around and kick the _____.

Tires (0)

Puppies (20)

When a colleague tells you about a personal triumph, you:

Sincerely congratulate them (–4)

Insincerely congratulate them and point out your own personal triumph (4)

"What were you saying? Triumph? What? Hey, can you hang on a minute? [muffled] Yeah, something about a triumph. Look, I guess I gotta take this. [back on the phone] Look, I have like twelve seconds to talk. You were saying?" (10)

Please fill in the blank: A rising tide _____ all boats.

Lifts (–2)

Who gives a shit? (10)

Please choose a location at the airport gate for waiting around 'til your boarding group is called.

Seat in gate waiting area (–3)

Right next to gate agent, one arm on desk (9)

Oh, just grabbing a bag of Chex Mix at the little shop over there (0)

You order the duck and the waitress says they're out of the duck. You . . .

Have the chicken (0)

Point out to the waitress that every time you come here you have the duck and why would the restaurant antagonize you like this, what with all the money you've spent here, and you just want the duck like you always have and have the chef make the duck, tell him it's you, he knows you, now, run along. (8)

Have you ever been drinking with two assistants after work and one of them asks you an innocuous question but it just sets you off and you make a scene almost like you had some negative feelings bottled up inside all because of your stress level?

That's really specific. (0)

Yeah, it sounds like you may be working through some stuff with this one. (0)

I'll accept that.

Cool. (0)

Cool. (0)

KEY

Fewer than 0 points: You are repressed and need to stop bottling up your emotions because some day they're gonna explode.

0–9 points: There's evidence that you experience the full range of human emotion, but your consideration for other people prevents you from being an asshole.

10–29 points: You are a son of a bitch.

30–50 points: You are an asshole.

More than 50 points: You are a sociopath.

47

The Case for Profanity

I'm not talking about how much profanity is *spoken*. I haven't seen the studies on profanity rates by geographical location, and I don't care what they say. I'm talking about how much is *heard*. I have spent time in many places, and nowhere will you hear the full tapestry of common—and not so common—vulgarities like you will in New York City. From the darkest corners of Bushwick to the benches of Washington Square Park to the hallways of an office building in Midtown, profanity is all around you. In places where people walk around instead of driving cars, you see and hear things you don't see and hear in other cities. Elderly women pushing elderly dogs in strollers for instance. You see that in New York. Elderly women pushing elderly dogs in strollers and yelling, "What the fuck, asshole?!" to a police horse. You see—and hear—that, too.

Profanity is a wonderful gift you can bestow upon the unenthused. And it's a useful thing—it can express emphasis and emotion that regular words simply can't. It can be used to great effect at the workplace as long as it's not used in anger. And so I hereby proclaim the following:

Whereas profane words express what other words cannot;
(There is no way to intensify something in the way that the word "fucking" can intensify it.)
Whereas profanity is funny;
(There are two ways to say, "Hand me that stapler," and only one of those ways is amusing.)
Whereas profanity grabs our attention;
(We tend to be surprised when taboos are broken.)
Whereas our brains process profanity differently than other words;
(Brain scans have revealed that profanity is processed in the "lower" regions of the brain and not the "higher" cerebral cortex, the brain's language-processing center. The theory goes that instead of processing an obscenity as units of sound that must be combined to form a word, the brain simply stores this emotionally loaded word as a whole unit. This difference may account for why we recognize and remember swearwords more easily than so-called neutral words.)
Whereas profanity physically affects us;

(Curse words have been shown to be "arousing"—causing our skin to perspire, for instance—and some researchers believe that curse words may even trigger something like a fight-or-flight response, releasing pain and stress-relieving endorphins, which would help explain why cursing can help relieve physical pain, as well as just make us feel better.)

Whereas profanity lends credibility to our speech; (This is what Joe Biden knows. A speech is a lot more memorable if it contains a well-placed "damn.")

Whereas profanity is the baseline, not the blip; (We are profane to the core. Our subconscious is a messy stew of "damn" and "shit" and "fuck" and "fuck you" and "fuck me" and "fuck that guy" and "fuck that guy's dog and his dog's mother that bitch." Only the prefrontal cortex of our brain keeps the curses, oaths, and obscenities from being vocalized. It shuts them down, sends them back to the pit from whence they came.)

Whereas the word "fuck" has more than 250 uses and variations alone (250!) and infinite possible variations;

Whereas profanity is our essential language, and in many ways it is our most powerful language;

Be it resolved that: Profanity may be used at the workplace, provided that . . .

1. It is used for intensity, not aggression. (Using it aggressively makes you a menace and a bully, and the utterance will forever be seared into the memory of all those present.)

2. Level 3 profanities be given preference. (In Level 1, you have your "fuck," "shit," "goddamn it," "asshole." In Level 2, you have your "Jesus Christ," "bitch," "dick," "piss," and the like. But in Level 3, you have your "son of a bitch," "bastard," "prick," "hell," and "damn." All of the fun, none of the crudity.)

3. It is used sparingly. (If you constantly use profanity, you're constantly crying wolf. It's the Yosemite Sam approach. You're just shooting off at the mouth. You seem unhinged, bouncing around, throwing your hat on the ground and stomping on it—if not literally, then metaphorically. When you actually want to enhance the substance of what you're saying, you're left without tools. Your curses no longer have the power to surprise. But if you want to be heard, if you want to startle or intimi-

date or get people to pay attention, a single curse can act like a grenade.)

4. All ne'er-do-wells be referred to as "jamokes." (Because there is no slur more colorful and amusing—and ultimately harmless.)

5. It furthers the goal—not sullies it—whatever the goal may be.

48

How to Work with Someone Who Clearly Resents You and Is Threatened by You and Would Prefer That You Weren't Around

I 'm not talking about assholes.

This is about a specific category of asshole. This is about the underminer. And underminers you can't let go unchecked.

Every workplace involves an underworld of politics and secret resentments. This is not a problem. It becomes a problem when someone who resents you begins to "undermine" you or "derail" you or "fuck up" your "shit."

I have encountered a handful of these people in my career and I'm always fascinated by their behavior.

The first thing to understand is: They might not know what they're up to. The subconscious might know, sure. But consciously they might be unaware that their behavior is unseemly. A 2014 Columbia Business School study found that people are awful at knowing how they come across to

coworkers. In studies where researchers set up mock nego-
tiations and then asked each participant to answer questions about their own assertiveness and their counterpart's
assertiveness, 56 percent of people seen by their counterpart as overly assertive thought they came across either un-
derassertive or appropriately assertive. We don't know how
we seem.

The first move is to try to figure out their motivations.
Maybe they lost a lot of money at the dog track, maybe their
father never said "I love you," maybe their underwear is
literally, somehow, in defiance of the laws of physics, in
some sort of wad. This will cut through your outrage and
recalibrate you back to the sympathetic human being you
are.

Once you figure out their motivations, refrain from
yelling, "I knew it! You son of a bitch!" and then quietly
sitting back down at your desk while your coworkers side-
eye each other.

You could confront them with the Basic Asshole In-
quiry. (See chapter 45.)

"Can I speak with you for a moment?"
"I've noticed that you _____."
"I'm wondering why you would do that considering
_____. Can you help me understand?"

But what's always worked for me is to address it in a casual but direct (and possibly funny) way as it's happening—maybe even in front of other people. Like this:

"Do you realize that you just totally edged me out of that conversation?"
"Do you understand that you're being a little, how do you say, abrasive?"
"When you look at me that way . . . are you going for churlish or tetchy?"

Then look at them the same as you would if you were walking down the street and saw a Chihuahua wearing a sailor outfit while walking on its hind legs.

You're going for "bemused."

You're not smiling. You're not frowning. You're just nonplussed. The series of questions implied by your furrowed brow is: "What's wrong with you? Why would you behave in such a manner? Where does one procure such a tiny sailor outfit?"

You don't want to take the "high road." Or the "low road." **The high road is way too safe and boring. The low road is a shit show. No, what you want is This Is the Way It Is Lane.** It's *lovely.* Treelined. There's a promenade going down the middle of it. Room for everyone to have a stroll or a jog. No annoying speed bumps. But no cops either. Just you pulling alongside another car, rolling down your window, and asking, "What are you up to, pal?"

Never kill them with kindness. Underhanded people don't respond to kindness, and psychologists say there's almost no evidence that it actually works. Killing with kindness is a passive-aggressive tactic that might work to momentarily dismay your counterpart, but, in the end, you haven't gotten anywhere. No, kill them with frankness.

The main thing is: Never fight.

You're going to regret doing battle. Because a battle can happen only when someone gets to win. But there's no *winning* at work. As longtime *Esquire* writer Tom Junod wrote in one of the best essays ever written, "A Philosophy of Fighting" (2011): "Anyone can win if they're willing to go far enough—if they're willing to win at the cost of . . . respect. The question is who can abstain from winning, who can resist the temptation of winning." Winning is what businesses do. Navigating is what businesspeople do. An interpersonal issue is never conquered; it's traversed.

The underminer must be disrupted. The offender has pushed things to a state of imbalance. Your bewilderment and deliberation will recalibrate the situation. The jerk will be either touched or flustered. Or a little of both. Even if you never get an answer to your question, you will have said: "I am watching you." And this will get you respect.

Are you being an asshole? Sort of. But your counterpart is being both an asshole *and* an underminer. And undermining requires a lot of extra energy that you're not having to expend.

You have the advantage.

49

"Two Beers and a Puppy": A Helpful Test for Determining How You Feel About Someone

"Two Beers and a Puppy" is a test that I developed while working on an *Esquire* story on the American "son of a bitch." The test is: In order to find out how you actually feel about someone, ask yourself, "Would I have two beers with this person?" And: "Would I allow this person to look after my puppy over a weekend?"

Some people are no and no. These people are to be avoided at all costs. Some people are yes and no. These people are to be cautiously trusted. Some people are no and yes. These people are no fun but they make the world a better place—for puppies, especially. And some people are yes and yes. These people are wonderful people and your life and work are better for having them in your life. Seek them out. Collaborate with them. Enjoy their company.

50

The Score

There are people who don't know the score, people who are trying to figure out the score, and people who don't know that there's a score. There are also the people who don't know the score but who think they know the score. These people are the worst.

The important thing is that you are aware that a score exists.

I am always trying to figure out the score in a business situation: where the power lies, what leverage people have, who's actually in charge. In a meeting, figuring out the score can be a kind of pastime. Some people doodle. I try to figure out the score.

Here's how a typical score-figuring process works:

Bullshit levels generally? . . . Moderate.

Bullshit levels from that guy? . . . High.

Why isn't she speaking? . . . Too junior . . . Fine.

Why isn't he speaking? . . . Probably has no idea what's going on . . . Worth factoring in.

Who's the most powerful person in the room? . . . Her.

Who thinks of themselves as the most powerful person in the room? . . . Him.

Who knows a good Thai place around here? . . . That guy right there.

Does the fact that he has taken two restroom breaks in forty-five minutes mean something? . . . Has to.

Is that a new haircut? . . . Perhaps.

Here is what I think I've learned in my many years of contemplating the score:

If you know more of the score than everyone else in the room, you are the most powerful person in the room.

The score is constantly changing.

The boss could know the score if he wanted.

The second-in-command usually knows the score.

The score *always* includes you.

You want to be as big a part of the score as possible.

If a coworker is all of a sudden dressing better this

week, then that person knows a little more of the score this week than last.

The best way to know the score is to talk to people in person.

When people are meeting behind closed doors, they have access to part of the score that you do not.

The amiable guy who doesn't come in early, doesn't stay late, seems relaxed, and just recommended to you an obscure Russian novella? Dude knows the score.

And here, for the first time, is The Score:

Facts × opinions – about how much salary everyone in the room probably makes – bullshit + knowledge of a good Thai place around here ÷ you = The Score

51

How to Forget About That Thing That Happened That One Time That You Still Wince About

A handful of classic concrete bad memories from my early time in New York still haunt me.

Like my first night in New York when I clammed up at dinner with my new colleagues.

Or the time I yelled at two assistants in a bar. (Note: You should arrive to work every day determined not to say or do anything that will make you send an email to someone tomorrow containing only the words, "Are we cool?")

Or the time a series of jokes fell flat during a talk. (If it's possible to bomb in front of colleagues, I've done that.)

These moments weren't disastrous. But they're too painful to forget and too minor to talk to a therapist about. It feels like those memories and other bad memories are like a colony of ants that, once disturbed by recollection, freak out and crawl all over my brain.

Here's what happens when you have an embarrassing experience:

Your brain's hippocampus begins processing the experience for long-term storage—that is, making a memory—which determines where it will be filed away. Experiences that are encoded as "implicit" memories (the information we recall subconsciously, like how to tie our shoes) are stored in one group of brain structures; experiences encoded as "explicit" memories (we have to recall them consciously) are kept in another. But because your gaffe comes weighted with embarrassment, it is encoded as an explicit *emotional* memory and tied specifically to the amygdala, a small almond-shaped structure where a lot of very powerful stuff is kept: fear, love, anger, desire.

The emotional component of your embarrassing memory makes it "sticky"—and research suggests that the more negative the emotion, the stickier the memory becomes. Psychologists who study memory, for instance, have found that painful childhood memories persist more than positive ones. This might be because we tend to dwell on negative events, which may help cement them more firmly into our memories. But there may be an evolutionary reason, too: Remembering pain and danger will make it more likely that we don't encounter things that are painful and dangerous. Such as a bear in the woods or an angry river or an audience of people who are not laughing at your shtick.

Hence the wincing.

The wincing isn't the main problem. The main problem is that the wincing is evidence of shaken confidence. And shaken confidence can lead to all sorts of undesirable outcomes, like nervousness during a speech or awkwardness when meeting people for the first time. There should be no wincing.

While these kinds of memories are difficult to shake off, they can be shaken off.

You could "change up" the memory.

This is similar to what Tony Robbins calls "neuro-associative conditioning," which involves defusing a bad memory by recalling it and then "scrambling" the details. The idea is to think of a memory and then picture it getting smaller, until it's like a movie playing on a tiny screen. Then try to fundamentally alter the memory by adding different information to it—picture someone walking a pot-bellied pig through the scene, for instance.

You could take the sting out.

Researchers have found that when subjects recall emotional memories (good or bad) and focus on remembering the *details*—what the room looked like, what kind of day it was, what they had for breakfast that morning—the emotions they feel are less intense and vivid, something that brain scans confirm. The details can "crowd out" the bad parts of the memory.

You could drink it away.

Actually, you can't. Or at least drunk mice can't, as shown in various experiments. My early experiences going to a bar almost every evening my first couple of years at *Esquire* can back this up. I felt better while I was drinking. But I didn't feel better the next day. And it turns out that all the booze was probably making me feel worse. Alcohol has a negative effect on cognitive processes.

You could banish it from your subconscious. You know: Suppress it.

(Now we're talking.)

Researchers have shown that people who actively try to block memories of a traumatic scene have a more difficult time describing it and remember fewer details from it. Other work has suggested that repressing memories can even help mute their *subconscious* influence.

So it's you versus your memories. If you're wincing, then you need to do battle with what is making you wince. It's OK to tamp it down, crowd it out, neuter it, alter it, suppress it, or stare at it until it gets uncomfortable and leaves, but you can't let it plague you.

There's too much work to do.

52

Why You Should Always Be an Outsider

I will never feel entirely comfortable being on the inside. I am never going to be as great as the great ones. There will always be someone better. There will always be a better version of me. The work I do will always be an inferior version of the work I could've done. This could be a crippling thing. But if we are aware that it exists and we understand its power, then self-doubt can become fuel.

When I first started in New York, I didn't think I was "ready for success." I didn't think I belonged.

But as I began to have small successes, as I began to get comfortable around people who'd previously intimidated me, as I began to be busy with work instead of anxiety, I found that "being ready for success" and "not being ready for success" are both part of the *same* condition. We are perpetually ready and not ready for success. Because success is constantly changing. What you consider success depends on where you are in your career. It depends on The

Score. It depends on how you just shook hands with that guy. It depends on how lunch went. It depends on how drinks went. It depends on that coworker one cube over who's loud-talking into the phone and letting everyone know he's accomplishing something, which makes you, if only for a moment, think that you should be loud-talking into the phone too. "Why don't I have anything to loud-talk about?" you think. You either stop worrying about the other person or you don't. It's up to you. You either let that bother you or you don't. But you're in control.

Even if you don't feel like you are.

Which is a feeling not entirely without benefits.

Feeling inadequate can force you to do your best work. It makes you research a problem more than you would if you were confident going in. It makes you prepare for a meeting more than the other attendees. It makes you try harder to be better.

The people I admire most are those who question their abilities even as they succeed. People who act as though their success wasn't preordained. People who think that things can still go wrong. I have always sought these people out at work. I rely on them. I support what they're trying to do. The people who act as if they have it all figured out have little to offer me because I have nothing to offer them. There's no growth. There's no learning.

We think of self-doubt as a hindrance, as a kind of deficiency. But it doesn't have to be a deficiency. When you have doubt, you have *more*. You have the problem *plus* doubt. You have more fuel, more reasons to work hard, more to prove.

More.

My first year at *Esquire* was spent waiting to be found out. I was sure I was a disappointment to the staff. I was sure I didn't belong. I was sure the whole thing was a big mistake. I was waiting to be told: "You're fired."

And then, really loudly: "Why were you here in the first place?!"

I used to walk over to Central Park after filing an edited story to my boss. I would attach the document to an email, click Send, and then immediately get up and walk out of the office. I figured you can't fire someone you can't find.

So off I went.

I walked two blocks north to Central Park, through the Merchants' Gate in the southwest corner, past the wall that I leaned on while studying my notes before my interview, past the long row of benches all the tourists sit in, down a hill, to a set of benches just south of the Sixty-Fifth Street Transverse that no one ever seems to use. Set inside an amphitheaterlike depression, the view these benches afford is mostly of the side of a hill and a small bridge. Not an expansive view but a green one. And a quiet place to sit.

Sitting there, I was inside the great expanse I saw out my airplane window. I was right in the middle of it. I walked over there during any kind of weather. Hot and humid. Snowy. Didn't matter. The point was not to be in Central Park. The point was to be out of the office. The point was to be out of my own head.

But being right in the middle of New York, right in the middle of Central Park, means being in a contradictory state. It's an oasis of tranquility bounded by chaos. It's a fantasyland. The retreat is oxymoronic. You are inside New York and outside it at the same time.

The metaphor was not lost on me, even then.

Over the years, I've visited those benches less and less frequently. As I became comfortable in my job and my city, as I became confident, as I came to realize that I was not going to be found out, there was less need for a retreat.

New York became less novel too. Instead of a cherished escape, Central Park became a bunch of trees I saw at the end of Seventh Avenue. Times Square became a place I told my cabbie to avoid. Fifth Avenue became a street I crossed on my way to Grand Central and not, for the love of god, walk down—especially during the holidays. Rockefeller Center became less of a movie setting and more of a welcome change of scenery on my walk to work. New York becomes less charged the longer you live and work there. Less weird. Less able to change your basic mindset. Less cinematic.

Now when I walk to those benches—once, maybe twice a year—it's to connect with the state I was in when I first moved to New York. It's a deliberate nostalgia. What I realize sitting there now is how important it is to feel like an outsider. It allows you to understand the connection between behavior and success. It forces you to *care*. It drives you to do better work. And I realize now that the crucial irony is that the outsiders are the ones that make the inside so rich and inspiring.

I realize now that I belonged from the very beginning.

Afterword

How to Write a Book in Which You Do Nothing but Tell Strangers What to Do

Sometimes you have to just insist that you are talented, driven, smart, funny, and wise. Look: No one is going to insist for you. No one. Oh, they might *endorse* you. They might bring your name up in a positive way. They might say, "Yeah, she's OK, I guess." But "insisting"? No, that's up to you.

I've found that the best way to write—magazine profiles, humor pieces, instructional essays, the book you're reading right now—is to assume authority. To claim knowledge of something, without apology. And to express yourself clearly and without hemming or hawing. (*Especially* hawing. A little hemming? Fine. But hawing? Dear god, no.) This is a bold move for a person who feels like an outsider. But this is what you have to do. You have to seize opportunities. You have to claim your authority.

For you: The book you want to write may be a metaphor for the job you don't think you can get, the raise you don't think you deserve, the responsibility you don't think you're ready for, the promotion you're afraid to compete for, the retort to a colleague's dumb idea that you don't think you're qualified to throw out there during a meeting.

But you have to insist to yourself and others that you're ready for these things. You have to tell your boss what you want. You have to say to your colleague that he's lost his mind. You have to boldly admit you don't know a cultural reference at a gathering of smart people. You have to confront someone who's undermining your efforts. You have to give a speech even though you're nervous. You have to write a book if you want to write a book. (Maybe write your book on an entirely different topic. I don't want you horning in on my territory here. A YA novel about mummy cheerleaders, perhaps. A chronicle of your year in some pleasant and charming European location ostensibly in order to absorb the gusto of its people. A book titled *Where'd My Nuts Go? What the Squirrels Can Teach Us.* Look, I don't know what you're into. It's your book.) The point is: You have to act. With gratitude, self-awareness, maybe a *tiny* bit of residual self-doubt that helps to keep you grounded, and a big smile that makes you feel a little stupid, you have to act.

Acknowledgments

To Kathi Reese, my aunt but also a mentor, who for some reason thought I might be interested in a little freelance work as a magazine researcher. . . .

To Susan Hicks and Chuck Thompson, who early in my career encouraged ambitions I didn't know I had. . . . To James Mayfield, my good friend and former coworker, who thought certain workplace customs were as absurd as I did. . . . To Chris Philpot, illustrator/animator/genius, who has remained my collaborator long after we were supposed to never work with each other again. . . .

To Elizabeth Spiller, a former English literature professor at the University of North Texas who stopped me outside the English building one afternoon to tell me that "From a Lass to Poor Yorick: Death in Olivier's *Hamlet*" was a funny title for a paper. . . .

To Amy Cosper, Carolyn Horwitz, and Jenna Schnuer

at *Entrepreneur* magazine, who are the best editors a columnist could ever hope to have. . . .

To Jenn Johnson, who researched this book and made it better than it would have been without her. . . .

To Jessica Renheim of Dutton, who expertly edited this book and whose impossible combination of enthusiasm and calm has been critically reassuring to me. . . .

To Daniel Greenberg of the Levine Greenberg Rostan Literary Agency, who kindly returned a vague email from an unknown writer and who eventually helped me understand what kind of book I should obviously write. . . . To Tim Wojcik of Levine Greenberg Rostan, whose attitude is *exactly* the kind of attitude you want by your side as you're walking around New York pitching your book to publishers. . . .

To Pilot, maker of the Precise V5 Extra Fine pen, and to Paper Mate, maker of the Mirado Black Warrior #2 pencil, both exceptional writing instruments. . . .

To the passengers on the Quiet Car of the 8:33 to Grand Central, who were important partners in the effort to write this book even though we have never spoken to one another . . . or even made eye contact, really. . . .

To my *Esquire* colleagues Peter Griffin, Helene Rubinstein, David Curcurito, Michael Norseng, Mark Warren, Richard Dorment, Tyler Cabot, Ryan D'Agostino, Peter Martin, David Katz, John Kenney, Bob Scheffler, Kevin McDonnell, Aimee Bartol, Darhil Crooks, Stravinski Pierre, Scott Raab,

Tom Junod, Tom Chiarella, Chris Jones, John H. Richardson, Mike Sager, Cal Fussman, Stephen Marche, A.J. Jacobs, David Wondrich, Nick Sullivan, Wendell Brown, Michael Stefanov, Jessie Kissinger, Lisa Hintelmann, and Anna Peele, who are each the best at what they do and who I've been honored to learn from. . . .

To Eliot Kaplan of Hearst Magazines, who happened to be flying out of Pittsburgh on Southwest Airlines that day and who began a chain of events that created the life I have now. . . .

To my boss David Granger, editor in chief of *Esquire*, who has taught me that great things can always be made greater. . . .

To Paula and Howie Myers, the world's greatest in-laws, who couldn't have been more enthusiastic, supportive, and helpful during the writing of this book. . . .

To Craig Teasley and Terry Pham, who, in defiance of the laws of genetics and filiation, are my brothers and who have, since we were kids, offered me crucial advice about life and work. . . .

To my father, Dan McCammon, a wise and funny man, whose unpublished treatise "I Have a Philosophy About That . . ." is obviously this book's antecedent. . . .

To my mother, Peggy Aston, who embodies integrity, humility, thoughtfulness, and grace and who has been and always will be my hero. . . .

Acknowledgments

To my wife, Nina, who brought her editorial talents to bear on this book and who allowed me to hole up and work on it every weekend for months and who makes me seem so much better than I actually am . . . and to my son, Theo, for, once or twice every Saturday and Sunday and at exactly the right times, flouting the "Don't disturb Daddy" edict by quietly opening the door to my office and smiling. . . .

Thank you.

Appendix 1

A Reading List: Self-Help Books That Are Not "Self-Help" Books

Despite my role in creating the book you are reading, I have not read a lot of self-help books—or at least I haven't read a lot of "self-help" books. Yet a lot of the books that inspired me over the last ten years *are* self-help books. They're easy to read. They're motivational. They contain lessons on how to navigate a career and life itself.

Moby-Dick, *by Herman Melville (1851)*

How to try the impossible . . . interrupted by excruciatingly tedious chapters on how to crew a whaling ship . . . But mainly: how to try the impossible.

Alone: The Classic Polar Adventure, *by Admiral Richard E. Byrd (1938)*

How to summon strength you don't know you have.

The Hour: A Cocktail Manifesto, *by Bernard DeVoto (1948)*

How to drink responsibly. As long as what you're drinking is a martini.

Hell's Angels: The Strange and Terrible Saga of the Outlaw Motorcycle Gangs, *by Hunter S. Thompson (1966)*

How to talk to people who don't really want you around.

The Right Stuff, *by Tom Wolfe (1979)*

How to be better than the best when you are the best.

Lonesome Dove, *by Larry McMurtry (1985)*

How to be a better business traveler.

What It Takes: The Way to the White House, *by Richard Ben Cramer (1992)*

How to compete.

On Writing: A Memoir of the Craft, *by Stephen King (2000)*

How to communicate with people. (Step 1: No adverbs.)

The Road, by Cormac McCarthy (2006)

How to go it alone.

Bossypants, by Tina Fey (2011)

How to do pretty much everything all at the same time.

WTF with Marc Maron podcast, episode 558 with actor-comedian Jenny Slate, from 54:00 to 119:00 (2014)

How to be grateful. (This is not actually a book, but who cares? Slate's chronicle of her difficult year as a cast member on Saturday Night Live is as moving a description of the experience of feeling like an outsider on as big a stage as I've ever heard.)

Appendix 2

How to Pronounce the Names of Scotches

The first time I ever had a drink with my boss in New York, I ordered a Dewar's on the rocks because I wanted Oban just like I'd been drinking at San Domenico, but I didn't know if it was pronounced "OBE-un" or "o-BAWN." So I ordered a Dewar's and prayed that it wasn't actually pronounced "dew-ARS."

That is a dumb thing to do. 1. It's not a big deal to mispronounce the name of a Scotch. 2. Oban is a much, much better whiskey than Dewar's.

I know it's a trivial thing: ordering a drink. But to me, ordering anxiety was just another way that I felt unsure. What should I order? Is this the right drink for this occasion? Should I eat this garnish? How do you pronounce "Bruichladdich"? Why should drinkers have to feel unsure about something so knowable? But where was the guide to how to pronounce Scotch? There wasn't one! But there is now, and it's the thing I am most proud of in my ten years at *Esquire* . . . OK, it's in the top ten.

The concept was simple: a short video for Esquire.com in which the brilliant and funny Scottish actor Brian Cox (*The*

Bourne Supremacy, Red, Adaptation, and the totally underrated *Super Troopers*) simply sits in a chair and pronounces the names of Scotches, which are of course difficult to pronounce because they typically involve fourteen times more consonants than words usually contain. The resulting video is simple, helpful, and strangely amusing. It's probably the most popular thing I've ever helped create at *Esquire* and I encourage you to go watch it on Esquire.com instead of reading the following list.

So, if you'll allow me, a guide to seemingly hard-to-pronounce Scotches. It may not be of any use to you, but it will be of great use to a nascent Scotch drinker. And that's no small thing.

AnCnoc: AH-nok

Auchentoshan: aach-en-TOASH-un (the "ch" is pronounced like the Scot's word "loch")

The Balvenie: Bal-VEN-ee

Bruichladdich: Brooch-LAD-ee (also like "loch")

Caol Ila: Cool-AYE-la

Glenfiddich: Glen-fidd-ikh

Jura: Joo-rah

Knockando: NOK-an-doo

Lagavulin: LAG-a-VOOL-in

Laphroaig: la-FROIG

Oban: O-bun

Tomatin: TOH-muh-tin

Tomintoul: Toh-min-TOWL

Appendix 3

Rules I Never Got To

If there are fewer than six other people in the room, shake everyone's hand. If there are six or more, shake approximately five hands and then nod amiably to the rest.

Look everyone in the eye.

Do not give out business cards before a meeting begins. Because it makes you look like a blackjack dealer.

Unless you're European, do not kiss anyone on the cheek. Especially twice.

No fist bumping.

Aw, what the hell. If you want to fist bump, then fist bump.

Don't carry yourself in a way that could be described as "jaunty."

Do not literally dance into a room.

At no time say: "Let's do this!"

When people introduce themselves, say their names back to them or take a mental note.

But try to keep their names in your head. Saying a person's name back to them twenty or thirty minutes after you've met them connotes graciousness and suggests respect and will endear you to them.

BCC says more about you than about the person you're BCC'ing.

Proposed new meanings for exclamation points:

!: This is so exciting.

!!: This is revolutionary.

!!!: I am literally about to pass out from excitement.

!!!!: I'm serious. I'm literally passing out right now.

!!!!!: Seriously, I'm in bad shape here. Call 911.

!!!!!!: No, wait. I'm feeling better. But seriously, this is really exciting.

Ending a statement with the phrase "and stuff" nullifies the statement's impact and substance.

In ascending order of forcefulness: email, face-to-face conversation, handwritten note, bear hug.

No bear hugs.

No squinting, which is threatening.

People who look away when answering a question are not to be trusted.

Never say you're swamped.

Or slammed.

Or overloaded.

Or being pulled in all directions.

Unless of course you are literally in a swamp or being slammed, overloaded, or pulled in all directions.

Saying "Uh-huh...uh-huh...uh-huh" in an indifferent fashion while texting does not suggest engagement in the matter at hand.

Laughter at some Instagram pic you just looked at does not suggest engagement in the matter at hand.

FaceTiming with Grandma does not suggest engagement in the matter at hand.

But it's the right thing to do and she really appreciates it.

Your general demeanor should be somewhere between ardent and fervent.

Sit up straight.

Straighter.

OK, now you're standing.

Sit back down and seem vigilant, attentive, for god's sake.

Never "float" an idea. Launch it, push it into the stream, yell at it with a bullhorn until it scowls at you.

Anticipate three different challenges to your idea. And have answers ready.

Platitudes are fine in a pinch.

Don't approach a social occasion as an intelligence-gathering mission.

When typing your witty rejoinder over Twitter, first go to the drop-down menu on the upper right and select "Sign out."

There's energy, and then there's ENERGY!!!

Energy involves eye contact, nodding, smiling, emoting, reacting, and moving on when things get bogged down.

ENERGY!!! involves fist pumping and the clapping of hands. Occasionally it involves jumping up and down on the conference-room table.

If there are doughnuts in the meeting, you must have a doughnut.

The cake doughnut is deeply underrated.

To determine if the person you can't stand is your enemy, say the person's name out loud.

If you are squinting and shaking your fist, then the person is your enemy.

If you are squinting, shaking your fist, and sneering, then the person is your archenemy.

If you are squinting, shaking your first, sneering, and stroking a white cat, then you are behaving like an evil genius in a James Bond movie, and you need to take it down a notch.

A flash of anger is like a comet: long, long tail.

Counting to ten works. It's a little infantilizing, but it works.

Counting to twenty works too. Takes longer, but it works.

Counting to thirty is a little much.

Four shakes of the hand will suffice. Anything more and it seems like you're trying to hold the other person until the police arrive.

No winking.

Or hugging.

Or hugging while winking.

No berating of a subordinate in front of others.

In fact, no berating ever.

Also: No berets.

No playful emails.

No scornful emails.

Slightly overdress.

If you don't feel nervous, it's not worth doing.

Appendix 4

Key Measures and Equivalents

8 ounces	1 cup
2 weeks	1 fortnight
1 workday	8 hours
8 hours	not enough time
glass half-full	glass half-empty
2 jerks	1 prick
3 pricks	1 son of a bitch
2 sons of bitches	1 asshole
!	Can you believe it?
!!	Seriously, can you believe it?
!!!	Seriously, can you believe it? + !
2 seconds of eye contact	1 smile
2 ounces of gumption	1 grit
grit + boiling water	grits
40 seconds of small talk in an elevator	weather + it's Friday
60 seconds of small talk in an elevator	weather + it's Friday + "Oh! I got your email!"
120 seconds of small talk in an elevator	stuck elevator
2 "Sincerelys"	1 "Best"

4 "Best"	1 "Yours"
6 "Yours"	1 "All my best"
1 "All yours"	basically a pickup line
1 pickup line	sexual harassment case
1 "All my sincerest best"	not a thing
1 tweet	.18 screaming out the window
4 waves	1 handshake
1 fist bump	seriously?
1 pat on the back	.0000008 pay raise
2 people or organizations + similar goals	synergy
4 synergies	1 emergence
1 emergence	total bullshit
1 upturned chin	3 stiff upper lips
bright side	1 bad attitude + 2 drinks
this book	blood + sweat + tears
blood	Actually, that's just a little ketchup. See? Wipes right off.
sweat and tears	Like, condensation or something. No big deal.
1 smile	1 frown turned upside down
4 smiles	1 wink
1 wink	creepy
7 butterflies	1 pang of self-doubt
4 pangs	you need to see a doctor

Index

About the Author

Ross McCammon has been an editor at *Esquire* magazine since 2005, where he's responsible for the magazine's coverage of film, TV, music, drinking, cars, and etiquette. He has edited *Esquire*'s "Dubious Achievement Awards" and the long-running annual feature "The Best Bars in America," writes the monthly feature "The Rules," and is a frequent contributor to the magazine's back-page humor section "This Way Out." For three years he has been the business etiquette expert at *Entrepreneur* magazine. His humor has been collected in *Created in Darkness by Troubled Americans: The Best of McSweeney's Humor Category*, edited by Dave Eggers. He lives in Westchester County with his wife and son.